The LIVES AND TIMES of THREE POWERFUL OJIBWE CHIEFS

Curly Head
Hole-In-The-Day the elder
Hole-In-The-Day the younger

Each in his own time was the principal Chief
of the Central Minnesota Pillager Ojibwe

by
Duane R. Lund
Ph.D.

Distributed by
Adventure Publications, Inc.
P.O. Box 269
Cambridge, MN 55008

ISBN 1-59193-027-8

Cover: Photos are of Hole-in-the-Day the Younger; there were no cameras
around during the times of his father and Chief Curly Head

THE LIVES AND TIMES OF
THREE POWERFUL OJIBWE CHIEFS

Copyright © 2003
by
Dr. Duane R. Lund
Staples, Minnesota 56479

Except for brief quotations embodied in reviews,
no part of this book may be reproduced in any
form without written permission of the author.

First Printing, 2003
Second Printing, 2004

Printed in the United States of America

Dedication

To the late David Nordell, founder
of Nordell Graphics.

With his encouragement and
expertise I became the author of
more than thirty books.

He was also a very special friend.

TABLE OF CONTENTS

Chief Hole-In-The-Day the younger

CHAPTER I
Geographic and
Historical Setting

CHIEF CURLY HEAD, CHIEF HOLE-IN-THE-DAY THE ELDER AND CHIEF HOLE-IN-THE-DAY THE YOUNGER ruled, in sequence, the same geographic area. Today we call it "Central Minnesota." More specifically, the area they ruled included all or parts of Aitkin, Crow Wing, Cass, Morrison, Wadena and Todd Counties. Each man, in his own turn, was recognized as "Principal Chief" of the Crow Wing, Gull Lake and Mississippi band of Ojibwe Indians.

Since water was the primary means of travel in those years, the area could also be defined as the portion of the Mississippi River between Aitkin and Little Falls, Pine River and the Crow Wing watershed which includes Gull River and the lower portions of the Long Prairie, Partridge and Leaf Rivers.

These Ojibwe were close allies of the Ojibwe villages farther north, including Sandy Lake (then capital of the Ojibwe Nation), Leech Lake, Cass Lake and Lakes Bemidji and Winnibigoshish. Our three chiefs, however, had no jurisdiction over any of these villages. All of these Ojibwe – both north and south were also called "Pillagers".

The area ruled by Curly Head and the Hole-in-the-Days was of tremendous strategic importance during the "100 Years War" (1739-1862) between the Dakota Sioux and the Ojibwe. There were two north-south routes of water travel through the Minnesota woodlands. Both routes passed through the area ruled by our three chiefs. The most often used north to south route was the Mississippi River going with the current. During times of high water when the current was strong, the preferred south to north route was a detour up the Crow Wing River, then the Gull River, Gull Lake, Round Lake, Long Lake and a whole series of short portages ending back on the Mississippi with access to such large lakes as Leech, Cass, Sandy, Bemidji and Winnibigoshish. In other words, if the Dakotas and Pillagers were to get at each other, they had to pass through the area of our study, the area ruled first by Chief Curly Head (1800-1825), then Chief Hole-in-the-Day I (1825-1847) and

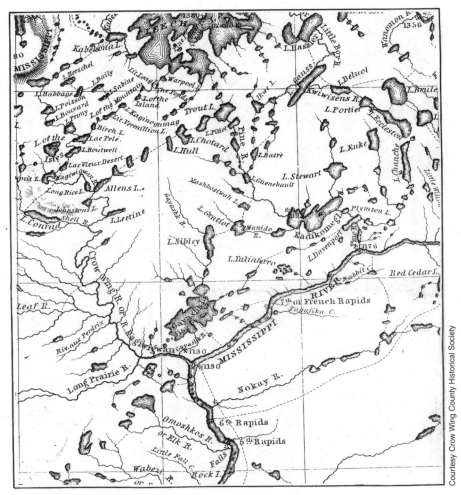

Joseph Nicollet's map of the area we will be studying. Gull River and Gull Lake are identified by the Ojibwe name, "Gayashk", meaning seagull. Nicollet was here in 1836; he was searching for the source of the Mississippi.

finally, Chief Hole-in-the-Day II (1847-1868).

During the reigns of our three chiefs this critical region was secured by the Ojibwe. There were permanent Ojibwe villages throughout the Minnesota woodlands. Although Dakota Sioux war parties from the Minnesota prairies tried again and again to penetrate the area, they were never very successful. The forces of Curly Head, and later of the two Hole-in-the-Days, were strategically located on the Mississippi, Crow Wing and Gull Rivers and Gull Lake and they were able to frustrate every Sioux attempt to invade the woodlands after 1800. Every time the Dakotas made such an attempt, or when they attacked the Ojibwe if they ventured south or west the Ojibwe chiefs and their allies launched punishing attacks of revenge from this stronghold. The Ojibwe were almost always the winners. In succeeding chapters we will narrate this military history as each chief, in turn, was involved.

THE COMING OF THE SIOUX AND THE OJIBWE TO THE AREA

To better understand this phase of the historic Sioux-Ojibwe conflict, we will take a brief look at how these two powerful tribes of American Indians arrived in the Minnesota woodlands in the first place.

The Sioux were here first, by more than 600 years. Yet, they were by no means the first tribe to come. Archeologists tell us that as the last glacier melted (the Pleistocene) Indian peoples followed it north. Who these very first residents were and where they went we do not know. Traces of tribes who lived here for a time or passed through have been identified as the Mandans, Assinaboin, Hopewell and Laurel. About 1000 A.D. the Blackduck tribe moved into the woodlands of what is now Minnesota. At about the same time, the Sioux moved into the prairie areas of the state. There are more than a dozen tribes within the Sioux Nation, but those who occupied the Minnesota prairies identified themselves as the Dakotas. They were closely related to the Lakotas and Nakotas who inhabited, and remain, in North and South Dakota. Another Sioux Tribe, the Mdewakanton, were in what is now southeastern Minnesota, but they were smaller in numbers and because of their location seldom encountered the Ojibwe. Although there were no doubt, problems and conflicts, the Dakota and Blackducks co-existed in the state for about 500 years. Then, in the early 1600s, the Dakotas took over the woodlands, driving the Blackducks north, into Canada.

Meanwhile, the Ojibwe, also called Chippewa or Anishinaubay, lived out on the east coast. They are just one tribe among several (eleven in all) that formed the Algonquin Nation. While the Ojibwe were in the east, the Iroquois were their historic enemy.

The Iroquois were among the first to acquire guns from the early white colonists and with this tremendous advantage drove the Ojibwe west on both sides (north and south) of the Great Lakes. Some sources claim that upwards of 10,000 Ojibwe were killed in the process. During the 1600's, the Ojibwe came far enough west to occupy what is now Wisconsin and an area north of Lake Superior, thus becoming neighbors to the Dakota Sioux.

As white explorers, accompanied by their priests, ventured westward they found the Ojibwe scattered over a large area, both north and south of Lake Superior. When missionaries arrived at Sault Ste. Marie in 1640, they found a sizable concentration of Ojibwe. This village grew to an estimated population of 2000 by 1680—a virtual metropolis by the standards of the northern tribes. After 1680 the Ojibwe moved farther west and the village declined in both size and importance. A new concentration developed at La Point – on Madeline Island at the mouth of Chequamegon Bay on Lake Superior. This new capital of the Ojibwe Nation eventually had a population of about 1,000.

The Ojibwe migration routes lead both north and south of Lake Superior; the majority chose the southern route and settled in Wisconsin. Those using the northern way settled along the north shore of Lake Superior and around Rainy Lake and Lake of the Woods. Contrary to what we might expect, there was little confrontation at first between the Ojibwe and the Sioux. The basic reason was economic. The French needed the furs of the Minnesota Lake region and knew virtually none would be available if the Sioux and Ojibwe were at war. The Sioux and the Ojibwe realized too that there would be no trade items available to them if they had to spend their time defending themselves against an enemy instead of collecting furs.

Du Luth was the chief negotiator and genuine hero of the peace-keeping effort. He wintered with the Ojibwe at Sault Ste. Marie in 1678-79 and during that time developed a good working relationship with both the French traders and the Indians. With the coming of the ice break-up in the spring, Du Luth led a band of Ojibwe to a site near the city which now bears his name, and there held a council with several tribes in an attempt to expand the fur trade industry into Minnesota and southern Ontario. At this meeting, representatives of the Dakota, Cree, and Assiniboine pledged friendship and cooperation with the French and Ojibwe. No mean accomplishment. Because there were so few French traders, the Ojibwe were to serve as middlemen, representing the French in trading with the Sioux and other tribes. It worked for almost 60 years. Du Luth also used the occasion to lay claim to the entire upper Mississippi area for France. In the same year (1679), Du Luth founded a trading post at Grand Portage on Lake Superior. From this base he established trade with the Sioux tribes of the lake region with the Ojibwe as the traders. Grand Portage was destined to become the rendezvous point for the voyageurs from Montreal ("porkeaters") and those from Lake Athabasca and other western points ("men of the north"). Because it was impossible to travel all the way from Montreal to the trading posts in the west and return in a single season, a meeting place was necessary for the exchange of furs and trade goods. Grand Portage was that place. This rendezvous, in July of each year, was an occasion for great celebration.

Trade developed rapidly. LaSalle reported in 1682 that the Ojibwe were trading with the Dakotas as far as 150 miles to the west of the Mississippi. The peaceful arrangement allowed large numbers of Ojibwe to settle in Wisconsin and along both the north and south shores of Lake Superior. But the peace was too good to last. The Sioux of the prairies (Lakota and Nakota) had not been included in Du Luth's conference and they frequently sent raiding parties into the Boundary Waters. By 1730 the truce was an uneasy one.

It was this testy atmosphere that greeted the French-Canadian explorer, Pierre La Verendrye, upon his arrival at Lake of the Woods in 1732. His construction of Fort St. Charles on the Northwest Angle of that lake helped keep the peace for a time, but the warpath which led from the plains of the Dakota to its terminal point at present day Warroad, on Lake of the Woods, was once again in use. La Verendrye, like other Frenchmen, allied himself with the Ojibwe, Cree and Assiniboine. It is not surprising, therefore, that the Sioux of the prairies eventually launched a direct attack on the French. The Lakota massacre on Lake of the Woods of twenty-one Frenchmen-including La Verendrye's eldest son, Jean Baptiste, and his priest, Father Alneau-really marked the beginning of all-out war between the Sioux and the Ojibwe and their allies, the Crees and the Assiniboines. In the same year, (1736) the Ojibwe gained a measure of revenge for La Verendrye by launching a raiding party from La Pointe into southeastern Minnesota. The Cree, Assiniboine and some Ojibwe had begged La Verendrye to lead an attack against the Sioux, but in his wisdom he refused. He knew that open warfare would bring more Sioux to that area and could very well mean the end for sometime to the fur trade business. His expedition was largely financed by Montreal merchants who had been growing more and more demanding for a better return on their investment. Without furs there would be no support from the East.

La Verendrye reminded the Cree, Assiniboine, Monsonis and the Ojibwe that it was the Lakota Sioux from the prairies of what is now North and South Dakota, not the Dakota Sioux of the woodlands, who killed his men. He addressed the Ojibwe in particular, pointing out the good relations they had developed with the Dakota Sioux as they brought them trading goods in exchange for furs. La Verendrye made it clear to all tribes that the French had no quarrel with the Sioux of the woodlands. His efforts were in vain as raiding parties were sent against the Dakota Sioux from what is now Canada and western Wisconsin. Within three short years after the Lake of the Woods massacre, the Dakota Sioux were dislodged from all of their Minnesota woodlands strongholds, including central Minnesota.

The first attacks on the woodland lakes of what is now Minnesota were not by the Ojibwe, but by their allies the Crees and Assiniboines from the north. Launching their attack from their Lake of the Woods and boundary water villages, they drove down on the Red Lakes, Winnibigoshish, Cass and then Leech. The Ojibwe seemed almost reluctant at first to join battle. Perhaps it was because their leadership still felt a loyalty to the French and their pursuit of peace among the tribes. However, when they had once committed themselves, it was with a vengeance. The Dakota villages at Sandy Lake were among the first to fall to the Ojibwe and their allies – and this site was to become the new capital of the Ojibwe Nation. Located on the watershed between Lake Superior and the Mississippi lake region at the end of the Savanna portage, it was the key to control of the entire area. The Cree were the first to establish villages on Leech Lake following the rout of the Sioux.

Thus, by 1739, the Dakotas had fled from their lake area strongholds and had moved their families to the prairies, and back into the southern part of the state – particularly along the Minnesota River. The once powerful Mille Lacs village of Kathio – what was left of it – was moved to the mouth of the Rum River. There also remained Dakota Sioux villages along the Long Prairie River and west of the Crow Wing River where the woodlands ended. As mentioned earlier, there were settlements of the Mdewakanton Sioux near present day Shakopee and Prairie Island, but with a couple of early exceptions, they were too far away to fight the Ojibwe. But the war was by no means over. It was really the beginning of a hundred year's war. No sooner would the Sioux be driven from an area than they would plan a counterattack. If the Ojibwe or their allies moved out of an area, the Dakotas moved back in. Sometimes old village sites were even resettled by the original Sioux families. Although the Dakotas had been driven from their strongholds, they certainly had not given up; nor were the Ojibwe and their allies strong enough to occupy and control the area. When villages were first established by the Ojibwe and their allies, they were often wiped out – including women and children. All of northern Minnesota soon became a virtual "no man's land" inhabited mostly by marauding war parties. The bands were not large – usually less than 100 braves in number. From 1739 to 1766, few tried to "live" in the area, and all who entered did so with intent to wage war. But when the ice went out of the lakes in the spring of 1766, the Ojibwe organized an army of about 400 warriors from their villages along Lake Superior and throughout Wisconsin. When the war party left Fond du Lac it was said that a man standing on a high hill could not see the end or the beginning of the line formed by the Indians walking in single file – as was their custom.

By mid-May, the better-armed Ojibwe had met and soundly defeated a much larger "army" of Dakotas, perhaps as many as 600 braves. The Dakotas at first fell back to Leech Lake and solidified their forces. Their first strategy was to occupy the islands of the lake. If they had been content to wait it out here until reinforcements arrived, they would have been relatively safe and could have held out for some time. However, over eager and over confident, the Dakotas made a grave error in strategy. They divided their forces and launched three simultaneous attacks on Pembina, Rainy Lake and Sandy Lake. They lost on all three fronts and the resultant disaster was the turning point of the war. The Sioux fell back to their villages west of the Mississippi and along the Minnesota River and they were able to keep their stronghold on the Mississippi at the mouth of the Rum River. As mentioned earlier, they were also able to keep their villages on the prairies west of the Crow Wing River and on the very upper portions of the Long Prairie River.

The Ojibwe were for the first time truly in control of the Minnesota woodlands and a serious effort was made to settle the area. Sandy Lake continued as headquarters for their operations but large villages soon appeared on the Red Lakes, Leech Lake, Cass Lake and Winnibigoshish. Even though the Ojibwe had effectively defeated the Dakotas, Sioux war parties would return again and again to view old village sites, visit the burial places of their ancestors and administer vengeance on the Ojibwe. In fact, if Ojibwe villages had not been replenished continuously with settlers from the east, they would probably have been annihilated.

There were significant battles in our central Minnesota area between 1766 and 1800 when Chief Curly Head established the first permanent Ojibwe village in this region, on Gull Lake.

A BATTLE AT THE MOUTH OF THE CROW WING (1768)

The Dakota Sioux had been driven from their villages in northern Minnesota just two years earlier, but had far from given up. They had been forced from their Mille Lacs Lake headquarters village when the Ojibwe blew up their earthen houses by dropping gunpowder down the smoke holes on to blazing fires. It was from their new headquarters village at the mouth of the Rum River that a small army of about 200 braves launched a raid against the new Ojibwe capital on Sandy Lake.

At the same time, an Ojibwe war party of about seventy men moved south down the Mississippi with the Rum River village as their objective. The Dakotas proceeded up the Mississippi (but chose to take the Crow Wing cutoff), they traveled up the Gull River, across Gull, Long and Whitefish Lakes, then up to Pine River and across a series of lakes leading to Boy River and Leech Lake – on the way to Sandy Lake (because there was less current to fight). Thus the two war parties did not meet on their way to their respective objectives.

Apparently the Ojibwe did not find any indication that the Dakota

Sioux had traveled north only days before. They were evidently totally surprised to find the Rum River village deserted, with the women and children safely protected elsewhere. Surprise turned to horror when the Ojibwe realized the possible significance of the empty village. Their worst fears were to be realized. The Dakota had fallen on a helpless Sandy Lake village and slaughtered everyone except thirty young women whom they took captive along with an older woman to care for them. The Ojibwe wasted no time looking for the hidden Dakota Sioux women and children but hurried back up river—intent on finding a battlefield of their liking to ambush the Sioux. They reached the mouth of the Crow Wing without encountering the enemy, and here they finally discovered camp signs left by the Dakotas on their way north. They dared go no further because they were not sure on which river the Sioux would come—the Crow Wing or the Mississippi. They quickly dug in on a bluff on the east bank of the Mississippi overlooking both rivers (where their excavations may be seen to this day as a part of Crow Wing State Park). They did not have long to wait. A scout reported that the Dakota Sioux war party was on its way down the Mississippi. They stopped across from Crow Wing Island, where they forced their captives to serve them breakfast, in full view of their loved ones who were anxiously lying in ambush.

The old woman whose life had been spared to care for the captives turned out to be a real heroine. She had quietly reminded her charges that there was a good chance they would meet the returning men from their village somewhere along the river. If and when this should happen, she urged the women to overturn the canoes and swim towards the rifle fire. And that is exactly what happened. The unsuspecting Dakotas were caught completely off guard and suffered heavy casualties. The Ojibwe had chosen their battlefield well. Here the Mississippi narrowed and made a sharp turn, the faster current bringing the Dakota Sioux into close range, but they were not about to give up their captives or leave without a good fight. Incensed over the sudden turn of events and the fact they had been outsmarted by their captives—women at that (Indian warriors of that time were real male chauvinists!)—they placed the Ojibwe under siege. When frontal attacks proved too costly, they crossed the river and circled behind them on land, but the Ojibwe were too well protected and continued to get the better of the battle. At last, the Dakotas decided "discretion was the better part of valor" and reluctantly turned their canoes down stream.

A BRIEF TRUCE

The only significant truce during the 100 Years War took place in the late 1770s when the Ojibwe and the Dakota agreed to hunt and trap in peace during the winter months in the area adjacent to the Crow Wing and Long Prairie Rivers.

These hunting grounds were among the best in the area we now call Minnesota. Elk, buffalo and beaver were in abundance, and there were also fair populations of deer and other fur bearing animals. When neither tribe was able to drive the other from the area, a winter truce was negotiated several years running. Prior to and after the truce, a hunter might very well return to his camp with a scalp or two hanging from his belt as well as furs taken during the day. The truce also made it possible for the entire family to move to the hunting grounds.

So good was the hunting, that the Ojibwe came from as far away as Leech and Sandy Lakes. These villages retained a close relationship over the years and it was their custom to rendezvous at Gull Lake or the mouth of the Crow Wing on their way to the winter hunting grounds.

The virgin pine forests of the north were not good habitat for wildlife because sufficient light could not filter through the heavy pine boughs to nourish the undergrowth which provided food for both animals and birds. Because of the scarcity of game in these northern forests and because of the thick ice covering on the lakes, it made sense to move to the edge of the prairies where food and furs were much easier to come by.

William Warren reported that the famous Ojibwe warrior and hunter, Noka, for whom the Nokasippi was named, in one day – starting at the mouth of the Crow Wing – killed sixteen elk, four buffalo, five deer, three bear, one lynx and a porcupine! He gave them to a trader who was spending the winter at the village of Crow Wing as his supply of meat for the cold season. Little wonder both the Ojibwe and the Sioux wanted to hunt here.

There were Dakota villages in the nearby prairie areas, but other Sioux, including the Lakotas, Nakotas and Wahpetons sometimes came here from what is now North and South Dakota.

Each fall, the Ojibwe villagers, as we have said, came up the Crow Wing and Long Prairie Rivers. After warring back and forth all summer, the only way the Ojibwe could be certain the winter truce would again be observed was to directly approach the Sioux villages and offer to smoke the pipe of peace. Dressed for the occasion and well armed, a vanguard – not so large as to be threatening but not so small as to be easy prey – would march right into the Sioux villages. The bearer of the peace pipe and the banner carriers led the procession. The customary response of the Dakotas was to welcome the Ojibwe with a volley of rifle fire. Sometimes the singing bullets were so near the ears of the visitors that it seemed the "name of the game" was to come as close as possible without scoring! Once it was clear that a truce was desired, the Ojibwe were welcomed into the lodges of the Sioux where they smoked the peace pipe and feasted on the best available food—sometimes literally beneath the scalps of their fellow tribesmen which may have been taken as recently as the past summer and now hung suspended from the lodge poles. The Ojibwe had a word for this ceremony; they called it "Pin-ding-u-daud-e-win," which is translated, "to enter into one another's lodges."

An interesting custom during these periods of truce was for warriors to adopt "brothers" from among the traditional enemies of the other tribes. Often they were considered as replacements for special friends or brothers lost in battle. There are many tales of adopted brothers being spared during subsequent raids or battles. It is told that the relationship between the two tribes sometimes became so friendly that there was intermarrying and even the exchanging of wives.

THE END OF THE TRUCE – CHIEF YELLOW HAIR'S REVENGE

Chief Flat Mouth of Leech Lake was the most able and significant leader of the Ojibwe in the 1800s. We will speak more of him shortly. His father, Wa-son-aun-e-qua or "Yellow Hair" however, was somewhat of a scoundrel. According to Flat Mouth, Chief Yellow Hair did not inherit his title, but achieved his leadership role through a remarkable knowledge of medicines, including poisons. It is said that his enemies lost their lives in a mysterious and unaccountable manner. His own son called him "vindictive" and "revengeful" and said that he retaliated against his enemies two-fold. It is likely that Yellow Hair was a follower of a well-known false prophet or "Shaman" of that day. This medicine man turned witch doctor garnered a tremendous following among the Ojibwe and persuaded them to forsake their traditional Midewiwin religion. He claimed to have a new revelation from the Great Spirit and urged all to throw away their little medicine bags and follow him. A religious rally of sorts was held at the location of present day Detroit. However, when it was discovered he could not raise the dead some of his followers had brought to him and when he was found hiding in a hollow tree when he was supposed to be in heaven conferring with the Great Spirit, his disciples (including Flat Mouth) deserted him.

Typical of Yellow Hair's vengeful spirit is the story of how the winter truce between the Sioux and the Ojibwe was broken:

As we have said, for most years during the previous twenty, a truce had been observed so that the two tribes could hunt and trap in peace during the winter. Also, as we have just mentioned, to cement the truce it had become the custom of individual warriors to adopt one another from different tribes as brothers. Yellow Hair and a Dakota Sioux warrior adopted each other and became friends. Yellow Hair, who already spoke some Sioux, perfected his mastery of the tongue. In the spring, just before their return to Leech Lake, four Ojibwe children, including Yellow Hair's oldest son, (Flat Mouth's brother) were murdered while at play by a marauding band of Sioux from the west.

Yellow Hair urged revenge. His followers and other Ojibwe chiefs felt this would be useless because the war party was long gone. Yellow Hair, however, argued for revenge against any available Sioux, including those with whom they had a peace treaty. Others urged moderation, and the chief finally agreed to return to Leech Lake with the bodies of the children. After burial, however, Yellow Hair and five of his warriors headed back for the Long Prairie River, intent upon revenge. They encountered the Sandy Lake band who were on their way home. The leadership of this group perceived Yellow Hair's purpose and tried to dissuade him, knowing that a resumption of hostilities would escalate making it impossible to hunt and trap in peace during future winters. They even gave him more than enough gifts to "cover" the death of his son. Yellow Hair accepted the gifts and pretended to return to Leech Lake. However, when they were out of sight, he again turned southwest.

William Warren in his "History of the Ojibways" described the eventual gratification of Yellow Hair's loss thus:

> On the head waters of Crow River, nearly two hundred miles from the point of his departure, Yellow Hair at last caught up with the two lodges of his enemies. At the first peep of dawn in the morning, the Dakotas were startled from their quiet slumbers by the fear-striking Ojibwe war-whoop, and as the men arose to grasp their arms and the women and children jumped up in affright, the bullets of the enemy fell amongst them, causing wounds and death. After the first moments of surprise, the men of the Dakotas returned the fire of the enemy, and for many minutes the fight raged hotly. An interval in the incessant firing at last took place, and the voice of a Dakota, apparently wounded, called out to the Ojibways, "Alas! Why is it that I die? I thought my road was clear before and behind me, and that the skies were cloudless above me. My mind dwelt only on good and blood was not in my thoughts."
>
> Yellow Hair recognized the voice of the warrior who had agreed to be his adopted brother during the late peace between their respective tribes. He understood his words, but his wrong was great, and his heart had become as hard as flint. He answered: "My brother, I too thought that the skies were cloudless above me, and I lived without fear; but a wolf came and destroyed my young; he traced from the country of the Dakotas. My brother, for this you die!"
>
> "My brother, I knew it not," answered the Dakota—"it was none of

my people, but the wolves of the prairies."

The Ojibwe warrior now quietly filled and lit his pipe, and while he smoked, the silence was only broken by the groans of the wounded and the suppressed wail of bereaved mothers. Having finished his smoke, he laid aside his pipe and once more he called out to the Dakotas:

"My brother, have you still in your lodge a child who will take the place of my lost one, whom your wolves have devoured? I have come a great distance to behold once more my young as I once beheld him, and I return not on my tracks till I am satisfied!"

The Dakotas thinking that he wished for a captive to adopt instead of his deceased child, and happy to escape certain destruction at such a cheap sacrifice, took one of the surviving children, a little girl, and decking it with such finery and ornaments as they possessed, they sent her out to the covet of the Ojibwe warrior. The innocent little girl came forward, but no sooner was she within reach of the avenger, than he grasped her by the hair of the head and loudly exclaiming—"I sent for thee that I might do with you as your people did to my child. I wish to behold thee as I once beheld him," he deliberately scalped her alive, and sent her shrieking back to her agonized parents.

After this cold-blooded act, the fight was renewed with great fury. Yellow Hair rushed desperately forward, and by main force he pulled down one of the Dakota lodges. As he did so the wounded warrior, his former adopted brother, discharged his gun at his breast, which the active and wary Ojibwe adroitly dodged, the contents killed one of his comrades who had followed him close at his back. Not a being in that Dakota lodge survived; the other, being bravely defended, was left standing; and Yellow Hair, with his four surviving companions, returned homeward, their vengeance fully glutted, and having committed a deed which ever after became the topic of the lodge circles of their people.

Fortunately, Flat Mouth differed in many ways from his father.

SIOUX FROM THE WEST ATTACK A FRENCH TRADING POST AT THE MOUTH OF THE PARTRIDGE RIVER

This account of the attack was also told to William Warren, the Ojibwe historian, by Chief Flat Mouth (the elder) of the Leech Lake Pillagers (Ojibwe); he was there.

One winter in the late 1780s, when Flat Mouth was a child and too young to bear arms, he accompanied his father, Chief Yellow Hair, along with other members of his tribe to the confluence of the Partridge (or Pena) and Crow Wing Rivers. A French trader had constructed a fort and trading post there just that fall. The Ojibwe called the trader "Ah-wish-to-yah", which means "blacksmith." Several voyageurs were with him at the time and together with the Pillager hunters and trappers totaled about forty men working out of the post. Most of the Indian men had brought their families with them, even though they knew there was a good chance of an encounter with the Lakota or Nakota Sioux. Dakota Sioux were in the area but at this time they enjoyed a winter truce with them. The trader was also aware of the danger but a heavy population of beaver had drawn him there. The concern about a possible attack was the reason a log stockade had been erected around the trading post and Ojibwe campground.

Late one night, ten Ojibwe Pillagers awakened those at the post with the alarming news that a sizeable band of western Sioux were in the area. The Ojibwe had crossed their trail and identified them by the lingering smell of tobacco (which was distinctly different from the tobacco of the Dakotas or the Pillagers, who seasoned their tobacco with the ground inner bark of the red willow (Kinnikinic). The Sioux (probably Lakota) were following a trail which would lead them to a small, defenseless camp of Pillager hunters. Craftily, the Ojibwe ran and circled ahead of the Sioux and crossed the trail they were following, hoping to lure them to the more easily defended barricade around the trading post. The strategy worked. By the time the Sioux arrived, the barricade had been reinforced and nearly twenty men, Pillagers and French, were ready for the attack.

The party of Sioux was large indeed – about 200 braves – but whereas the men at the post were armed with guns, the Sioux were forced to depend on bows and arrows and had only about a half-dozen rifles among them.

The huge war party finally appeared on the riverbank across from the trading post. Confident in their numerical superiority, they leisurely put on their paint, feathers and other ornaments. Then, sounding their war whoops, they charged across the ice sending a cloud of arrows into the fortification. But the defenders were well protected and their rifle fire was devastating. No Sioux warrior reached the barricade. With a change in strategy, the attackers began firing their arrows almost straight up, lobbing them – like mortar fire – into the compound. The shower of barbed missiles was more effective and two Ojibwe hunters were wounded seriously enough to take them out of action. Some took refuge in the post itself. But in the end, the rifles proved to be more than an equalizing factor and a frustrated Sioux war party – with a greatly diminished supply of arrows – finally realized the futility of the situation.

Before leaving, they cut holes in the ice and gave their dead a watery

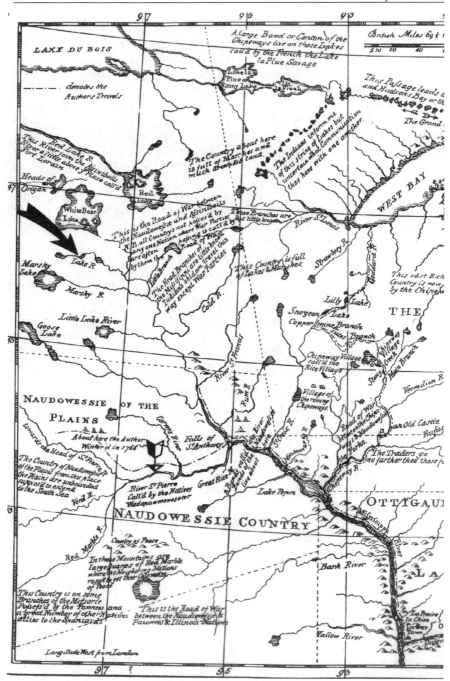

Jonathan Carver's map of what is now Minnesota – based on his explorations in 1766 and 1767. The large black arrow near the left margin marks the Crow Wing River. He calls it "Lake River". The Marshy River is the Long Prairie. White Bear Lake is probably Leech Lake. In the upper left hand corner is the Lake of the Woods. Carver identifies the Sioux as the "Naudowessie".

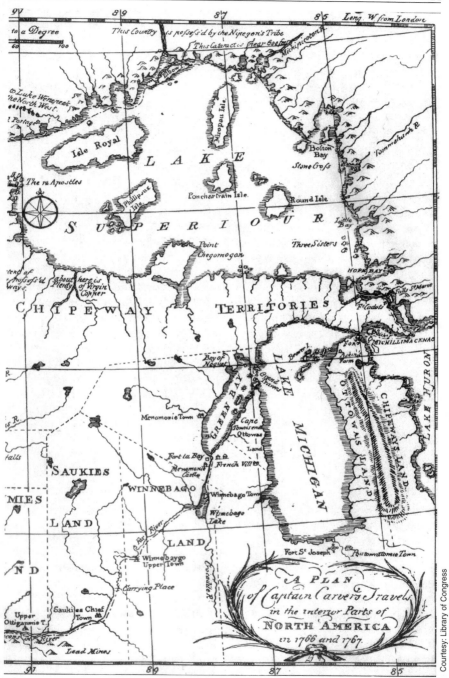

burial. This was done because they feared the Pillages would scalp their dead comrades after they left and they believed they would then enter their "Happy Hunting-ground" without their hair.

Shortly after their departure, other hunters and trappers who had heard the shooting arrived at the post – about twenty reinforcements in all. Realizing that the Sioux were nearly out of arrows, they wanted to press their advantage and pursue them. The trader argued to the contrary and prevailed. It is interesting that at this date – the early 1780s – the Sioux from farther west had so few guns.

The trading post stood on land that later became the village of Old Wadena.

CADOTTE WINTERS NEAR THE MOUTH OF THE LEAF RIVER

John Baptiste Cadotte, more than anyone else, opened the Minnesota Lake Region to the Northwest Company fur traders. Following his graduation from college in Montreal, he received a legacy of 40,000 francs from his father. With this capital he entered the fur trading business.

In 1792 he organized a large expedition for the purpose of exploring the sources of the Mississippi River and carrying on trade as he went. Actually, he divided his expedition into several contingents. The group under his leadership proceeded down the Mississippi, up the Crow Wing and then, because of all the signs of beaver, decided to winter on the Leaf River, just a short distance up stream from its mouth. Other units wintered at Prairie Portage on the Red River and at Pembina. A large number of Leech Lake Ojibwe traveled with Cadotte.

A number of women were included in the Cadotte expedition, but because they were going to be close to Sioux territory, most of them were left at Fond du Lac for the winter.

About a half-mile from the mouth of the Leaf, on the north side of that river,* Cadotte and his crew erected several log cabins and surrounded them with a stockade. Hunting was good and a winter's supply of buffalo, elk, bear and deer soon were in store. Once the camp was secure, Cadotte sent his men out to trap and hunt.

Early one morning, a large party of Sioux appeared in battle dress. With war whoops they advanced on the stockade, and once in range, showered it with arrows and discharged the few guns they had in their possession. Even though two of his men were wounded, Cadotte ordered that no one should return fire, instead, he raised the British "Union Jack" for identification and a white flag, indicating he wanted to talk.

The Indians ceased their attack, and after a brief consultation, a number of braves approached the gate. Cadotte stood in the opening and spoke through an interpreter, a man named Rasle. He told them he had

*We are not sure of the exact location; some think it was actually on the Crow Wing.

not come to wage war, but to trade. The Sioux accepted this explanation and replied that they had thought they were a band of hostile Ojibwe. (This took place after the Dakota-Ojibwe winter truce had been broken). They offered to smoke the pipe of peace. Cadotte invited the chief and other leaders into his cabin, while his men kept an anxious eye on the Sioux who remained outside.

Cadotte gave the Indians presents of tobacco, meat and ammunition. The Sioux, in return, insisted that he go with them to their village, about a day's travel away, where they said they had many beaver skins. Cadotte agreed. He took with him thirty of his best men. Well armed, and carrying packs of trade items, they returned with the Dakotas to their village.

The camp proved to be a large one – over one hundred lodges. The Whites were well received and feasted on choice cuts of venison, elk and bear. Cadotte was housed in the chief's own lodge, where he set himself up in business and traded with a continuous stream of Indians all that night. By morning he had all the beaver skins his men could carry. Unfortunately he had many trade items left over. This fact apparently upset the Dakotas who had few contacts with traders and did not want to see all these treasures leave their village. At any rate, they plotted an ambush on the return trip.

As Cadotte and his heavily laden voyageurs left the village, they were accompanied by the Chief and a number of warriors. Rasle, the interpreter, noted that there were no men in the village when they left that morning – just those who accompanied them. About half-way back to the stockade, just short of a heavily-wooded area, the chief indicated that he and his men wanted to rest and smoke awhile but that the Whites should go on ahead with their loads – and they would soon catch up. At this point, Rasle relayed his suspicions to Cadotte – suggesting that an ambush lay ahead in the grove of trees. The trader reacted quickly by placing the barrel of his revolver against the chest of the chief. Others disarmed the outnumbered warriors. When the chief realized that the truth was out, he wept for his life and the safety of his men. On Cadotte's orders, he sent one of his braves ahead and soon a small army of Sioux warriors fled out of the wooded area and headed back to the village. Cadotte took the chief and his men to the stockade as hostages until he could warn his men and the Pillagers that the Sioux could not be trusted and to be on guard. When he finally released the Dakotas, he again gave them presents – in the hope whey would be willing to "let by-gones be by-gones" and enjoy a peaceful co-existence. It worked. The Dakotas were not seen again near the stockade or in the area where Cadotte's hunters and trappers were harvesting furs.

The trader's journal also revealed a tale of tragedy in late winter –

perhaps the result of "cabin fever." A voyageur named Bell was accompanied by a huge black servant called "Negro Tom." One night with both had been drinking heavily the two got into a fight and the black giant soon had Bell on the floor. The white man's Indian wife was present, and fearing for her husband's life, attacked Tom with a knife and killed him. The big bones of Negro Tom are buried in an unmarked grave near the mouth of the Leaf.

That spring, Cadotte's expedition broke camp and continued up the Leaf River. They eventually portaged into Ottertail Lake and from there worked their way west to the Red River and then downstream, North.

We know that Cadotte's fort was near the mouth of the Leaf River. Because river channels do change we can't be totally certain that the river today is as it was in his time. There is a piece of high ground about a half mile upstream from the mouth of the Leaf on the north side of the river that appears to be the most likely location. The village of Old Wadena, which came into existence much later, must have been very close to the Cadotte fort.

The location of the Sioux village is unknown, but it was a day's journey west of the Cadotte post and on the prairie.

Here is probably as good a time as any to tell the story of HOW THE CROW WING, CASS, LEECH AND CENTRAL MINNESOTA OJIBWE CAME TO BE CALLED "PILLAGERS."

This was not a battle between the Ojibwe and the Sioux, but it was a significant incident in our area's history. It took place at the mouth of Pillager Creek, where it enters the Crow Wing.

Because of the inter-tribal wars, few traders had ventured into the woodlands area for many years. In the spring of 1781, a trader, accompanied by a handful of voyageurs, traveled up the Mississippi. He chose the Crow Wing cut-off and camped at the mouth of what is now called Pillager Creek. Here he took ill and was forced to rest. A band of Leech Lake Ojibwe—perhaps out to make sure there were no Sioux war parties in the area—had traveled down the Gull Lake-Gull River route and came across the sick trader and his men. They were most anxious to do business. The trader, unfortunately, was too ill to negotiate. The young braves, however, were not to be denied.

As the story goes, they at first intended to leave items of equal value to those taken, but when a cask of "firewater" was discovered and consumed, their judgment was clouded. As matters grew worse, the voyageurs placed the trader in his canoe and headed back down the river. The next day, near the present site of Sauk Rapids, the trader died.

It is said that the Leech Lake Ojibwe came to be known as the "Pillager Indians" because of what happened here. Even other Indians called them "Muk-im-dua-Wine-Wug" which means those who take by force. The city, the creek and the tribe all receive their names from this incident. Even treaties with the U.S. Government use the word "Pillager". Because Chief Curly Head and his village came from the Leech-Sandy Lake area they could legitimately be called Pillagers but they are also referred to as "Ojibwe" or "Mississippi Pillagers" or "Mississippi Ojibwe".

In this book, when we speak of Ojibwe, Pillagers, Mississippi Indians or Anishinaubay, we are talking about the same people.

THE HISTORICAL IMPORTANCE OF OUR CENTRAL LAKES AREA

As we have seen, the Central Minnesota area was of great military significance in the struggles between the Dakotas and the Ojibwe. The area also had historical significance in the growth and development of the state during the regimes of Curly Head and the two Hole-in-the-Days:

- The village of Crow Wing sprang up on the Mississippi across from the mouth of the Crow Wing River. In its prime it was one of the largest settlements in the state and home to several prominent political leaders, including Henry Rice, our first United States Senator; and William Warren, who served in the Minnesota Territorial Legislature and wrote "The History of the Ojibways."

- The village of Old Wadena appeared on the Crow Wing between the mouths of the partridge and Leaf Rivers. It served travelers on the Red River Woods Trail and according to one report had a population of about 100.*

- The Woods branch of the Red River Ox Cart Trail ran through the area from the village of Crow Wing to Ottertail. Without the permission and help of the Ojibwe it would never have been built or used.

- The Winnebago (Ho-Chunk) reservation was headquartered at Long Prairie from 1848 to 1855. Not only did it have a large Indian population, but there were many Whites living there as well. The total population was more than St. Paul at that time and Minneapolis didn't even exist.

- Because of the Winnebago reservation, Fort Ripley was built, and because of the reservation, the second road in Minnesota was constructed, joining the reservation to the first road built, which followed the Ox Cart Trail between the village of Crow Wing and Fort Snelling.

Travelers on the trail and Ojibwe may have contributed to this total. Census data and other reports indicated less than twenty permanent white residents.

MINNESOTA IN 1852

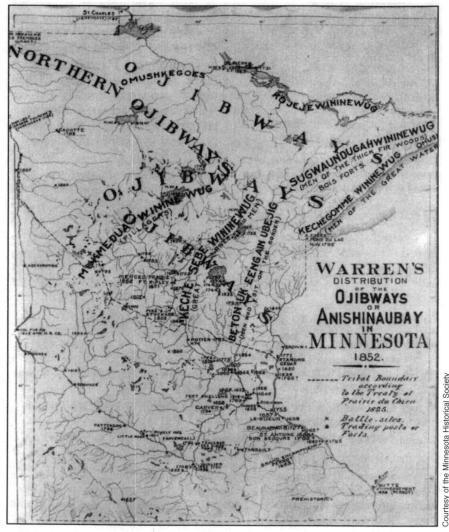

William Warren's map shows the location of the several Ojibwe "sub-tribes", including the Pillagers, in 1852. Note the dotted line separating the Sioux and Ojibwe territories as agreed in the Prairie du Chien Treaty of 1825.

- With the permission of the Hole-in-the-Day II, the second area in the state to be logged was Central Minnesota – along the Crow Wing River and its tributaries and then the Gull Lake area and the nearby Mississippi.

- The first missionary outreach to the Indian peoples of Minnesota was to the Long Prairie Winnebagos and a little later to the Ojibwe on Gull and Mission Lakes.

- At the same time as the Sioux Uprising in the Mankato-New Ulm area in 1862, Chief Hole-in-the-Day the Younger, considered collaboration with the Sioux and threatened to kill the Whites in Northern Minnesota and did burn down the missions on Gull and Lower Mission Lakes.

- There was an historic exodus of Ojibwe to White Earth when the Gull Lake Reservation was closed.

These and many other incidents will be discussed as we meet the three charismatic chiefs. Thus, our Central Minnesota region, the area ruled by Chiefs Curly Head, Hole-in-the-Day the Elder and Hole-in-the-Day the Younger, was truly a focal point of Minnesota history during their collective reigns from 1800 to 1868. When Curly Head moved his people from Sandy Lake to Gull Lake in 1800, the area we now know as Central Minnesota was pretty much wilderness. The population was probably more than 99% Native American. There was only a handful of white traders and an occasional explorer. The area west of the Mississippi River was still owned by France.

When Hole-in-the-Day II was assassinated in 1868, Minnesota had become a state, the Civil War had been fought, white settlers had arrived in Central Minnesota and Indians were being moved onto reservations. These three powerful men truly had a major impact during the development years of this area and of the State of Minnesota.

CHAPTER II
Chief Curly Head
(Ba-be-sig-undi-bay)

A word or two of caution is in order as we begin our discussion of the three dynamic Pillager chiefs. There will be a temptation to judge them by our culture, present day laws and our standards of behavior. Each did things we might consider violent and/or uncivilized. Yet, in their day, these acts may have been commonplace in all or nearly all American Indian tribes. They were part of the culture of that day. There were times when it was a matter of kill or be killed. And certainly there are plenty of atrocities today in our so-called civilized world that make their deeds seem less out of the ordinary.

American Indian culture and white culture still have their differences, and that is not to say either is right or wrong. For example:

property
Indians tend to think in terms of communal ownership while Whites stress ownership by the individual.

time
Indians think more in terms of the changing seasons; or monthly moons; Whites are "clock watchers." Indians say that meetings will start "when we all get there"; Whites say "the meeting will start at 1:00 sharp and be on time."

formality
Indians tend to be more informal; Whites are more formal and systematic.

cooperation vs. competition
Indians stress cooperation; Whites are more competitive. Even in games, Indians traditionally played more for the fun of the activity while Whites may be more concerned about winning.

family

Indians think in terms of the extended family, which includes aunts, uncles and cousins. Whites tend to focus more on the immediate family.

elders

Indians have a high respect for their elders and individuals tend to become more influential and more respected as they grow older. As Whites retire or grow old they tend to have less influence.

nature

Indians think of themselves as close to or even a part of nature. Whites may tend to be more interested in technology and other creations by humans and consider nature to be a gift of God for their personal enjoyment.

materialism

Indians teach their children to share with others and the accumulation of this world's goods isn't very important. Whites are more possessive and consider the accumulation of wealth as one way of elevating their status in the eyes of others or of measuring success in life.

history

Indians have long relied on oral history; passed down from generation to generation; Whites tend to distrust oral history and are more inclined to believe the printed word.

assertiveness

Indians tend to be more passive; Whites more aggressive.

eye contact

Indians consider it disrespectful to look someone in the eye; Whites believe eye contact improves communication.

Another word of caution: much of what we know about the three chiefs, particularly the Hole-in-the-Days, is from the writings or reports of the Whites of that day who were in conflict with them.

The chiefs seemed to get along well with other Ojibwe leaders, with a couple of exceptions. Chief Bad Boy of Mille Laces Lake was originally a chief on Gull Lake and a neighbor of Hole-in-the-day II. Part of the problem may have been that Bad Boy was particularly friendly with the Whites. For example, he provided the land on which the St. Columba mission was built. Several years later Hole-in-the-Day burned it down. When three of Hole-in-the-Day's young warriors murdered a white peddler on the shores of Round Lake, Bad Boy captured them and turned them over to the sheriff in the then tiny village of Little Falls. Then, when the United States Government reaffirmed Hole-in-the-Day as principal chief of the Gull Lake-Crow Wing-Mississippi Ojibwe, Bad Boy moved his people to Mille Lacs Lake, out of the principal chief's jurisdiction. Finally, in 1862, when Hole-in-the-Day threatened to kill the Whites living in northern Minnesota, Bad Boy sided with the Whites and threatened to fight against the Gull Lake chieftain.

The only other record we have of discord among the Pillager chiefs was also in 1862 when Hole-in-the-Day threatened to kill the Whites in the area. Near the end of the threatened conflict, the Leech Lake leadership disassociated themselves from Hole-in-the-Day and went home in a huff.

John Johnson (Emnegahbouh), the Ottawa deacon of St. Columba Mission, wrote in very negative terms about the younger Hole-in-the-Day; this is understandable since the chief threatened to kill Johnson on several occasions and did burn down his church.

Although all three chiefs and their braves killed many Dakota Sioux, there is a record of only one White being killed by them—the merchant to whom we have just referred.

Even among the other Ojibwe in what is now Minnesota, there is a record of only five Whites being killed by them: a trader at Red Lake in 1905, another trader on Lake Pepin in 1824 and three traders on the Mississippi who were mistaken for Sioux.

Both Hole-in-the-Days, especially the younger one, made threats to kill Whites but never carried them out. To the contrary, there were many times the Whites were befriended by the chiefs and for the most part, the Pillagers and the white traders and settlers lived in harmony.

The Dakota Sioux, on the other hand, killed Whites on several occasions, including the nearly 500* who died in the Sioux uprising in 1862. On many occasions, it was the Ojibwe who protected the Whites.

As stated earlier, the Ojibwe, in 1766, were finally successful in driving the Dakota Sioux from the woodlands of what is now Minnesota. Following that date, attempts were made to establish villages in the conquered territory. This was done with great difficulty because Sioux raiding parties returned north again and again and would sometimes annihilate entire villages. Men, women and children were all killed. Sometimes, however, young women were taken as slaves.

As more and more Ojibwe migrated into the area from both south and north of Lake Superior, the settlements finally became more secure. Curly Head was among the Ojibwe who first settled on Sandy Lake. He was of the Crane Totem (Bus-in-as-see), one of the largest sub-tribes of the Ojibwe nation. Most people of the Crane Totem lived along

*We do not know how many Dakota Sioux were killed; possibly many more than 500. It is highly probably that more American Indians were killed by Whites than visa versa in early Minnesota history.

the south shore of Lake Superior, which just might explain Hole-in-the-Day and Strong Ground's connection with Gull Lake, since they originally came from a Lake Superior village and were also of the Crane Totem.

We don't know exactly when Curly Head arrived at Sandy Lake or how or when he received the rank of chief. We do know he was a part of the leadership on Sandy Lake in 1800 when it was decided that permanent villages needed to be established farther south to secure the entire woodlands area against Dakota Sioux war parties. Since Gull Lake was a strategic location on the alternate (to the Mississippi) canoe route north, it was chosen as the site for one of these permanent settlements. Curly Head and his people either volunteered or were chosen to move there.

The northeast corner of Gull Lake was selected as the village site, perhaps because what we now call Dutchman's Bluff provided a perfect view of most of the lake. Any effort by the Dakotas to use this route would be totally visible. Previously, the bluff may have been a Sioux village and a Blackduck site before that. Curly Head remained here until his death in 1825 and was successful in preventing the Dakota Sioux from using this south to north canoe route. Later, villages would be established with sub-chiefs on both Mission Points, Gull (formerly Squaw) Point, Sand Point and the parcel of ground between Gull, Round and Long Lakes. Curly Head was recognized by both the Indians and the Whites as the principal chief of what is now Central Minnesota.

Curly Head was characterized to the author, William Warren, thus: A gifted leader, "He was a father to his people. They looked on him as children do a parent; and his slightest wish was immediately performed. His lodge was always full of meat, to which the hungry and destitute were ever welcome. The traders vied with one another who should treat him best, and the presents which he received at their hands he always distributed to his people without reserve. When he had plenty; his people wanted not."

Both the Pike and Cass Expeditions visited Curly Head and each honored him with a medal and an American flag.

Curly Head was contemporary with two other great Ojibwe chiefs: Flat Mouth (Eshke-bog-e-coshe) of Leech Lake and Broken Tooth (Ka-dow-aub-e-da) of Sandy Lake. The latter was son of Bi-aus-wah, who led the historic invasion of the Minnesota woodlands against the Sioux in 1766.

Curly Head and Flat Mouth joined forces on at least one occasion to wage war against the Dakotas. A raiding party was organized to avenge the deaths of Flat Mouth's nephew and two of Curly Head's allies—Waub-o-jeeg II and She-shebe. The latter two and their families were killed and scalped while fishing through the ice on Mille Lacs Lake. She-shebe is remembered for his heroic efforts at Battle Point on Cross Lake, where a camp of Ojibwe returning from their winter hunt were ambushed and nearly annihilated (1800). The Sioux war party reportedly consisted of nearly 400 braves while the Ojibwe, according to their report, had only half that number, including women and children. Waub-o-jeeg was a war chief for Curly Head.

Flat Mouth's nephew was killed by the Dakotas after the Mille Lacs Lake incident and it was his death that motivated Flat Mouth to join forces with Curly Head in teaching the Sioux a lesson.

A large war party from Leech Lake joined a Gull Lake contingent on the

Chief Flat Mouth of Leech Lake, an ally of Curly Head. Profile view of the statue on permanent display on the third floor of the Senate Wing in the United States Capitol.

Crow Wing. There were probably about 200 warriors in all. They traveled up the Long Prairie River, which enters the Crow Wing just south of present day Motley, until they reached a Dakota Sioux village of about 40 lodges. The Ojibwe were undetected and surrounded the village under cover of darkness. They attacked at dawn with the advantage of complete surprise. The Dakotas fought bravely but suffered heavy casualties in the initial attack and were under-manned to start with. The battle raged all day; in the end, only seven Sioux survived. Flat Mouth and Curly Head were satisfied that the deaths of their relatives and friends had been avenged and the seven were allowed to live—reportedly out of respect for their bravery. The Ojibwe left with the coming of darkness, but not before killing all of the Dakotas' horses. The animals were of little value in the woodlands where water transportation was more efficient.

This incident is an example of how Native American Tribes weren't very selective in taking revenge. If the culprits weren't available, revenge was taken on other villages of that tribe.

As an interesting sidelight, a ten-year-old boy tagged along with the Gull Lake contingent. He hid himself during the battle, but when he spied a wounded Dakota Sioux, he rushed in and finished him off, taking his scalp home as a trophy. The young lad became known later as

Chief Strong Ground, older brother of Hole-in-the-Day the first!

Thus we know that Chief Curly Head knew the brothers, Strong Ground and Hole-in-the-Day the Elder long before they arrived at Gull Lake with the Cass expedition. As we shall explain later, young Hole-in-the-Day in particular played a critical role in not only saving the expedition but probably saved their very lives as well! Curly Head was so impressed with the young brothers he appointed them as his pipe bearers – a rank often leading to becoming a chief.

It was probably after receiving this honor that Hole-in-the-Day and Strong Ground, along with a third and younger brother, "the Branch", Zhegud, further impressed Curly Head. The occasion took place during a temporary truce between the Dakota Sioux and the Ojibwe. Curly Head and a relatively small number of braves from his Gull Lake village were on the Mississippi in, or close to, Sioux territory. A band of Dakotas, who apparently were not aware of a recent truce, captured them. It is surprising that they did not kill them all on the spot but chose to take Curly Head captive and let the others go. They brought him back to their village with intent of publicly killing him. Fortunately, a Dakota warrior – possibly a sub chief - from a neighboring village saved his life. He apparently knew Curly Head well. We haven't a clue as to how. At any rate this unknown hero persuaded his fellow Dakotas that killing Curly Head would mean all out war. After presenting a number of gifts to the village he was allowed to escort Curly Head back to safe Ojibwe country.

When Hole-in-the-Day, Strong Ground and their brother, The Branch, heard of the incident, they swore revenge. The three of them chose Little Crow's* village, located about 20 miles downstream from St. Anthony Falls, as their point of attack. After leaving their canoe at the falls, they approached the village at night. They carefully laid a false trail to lure the Sioux, after their attack, in the wrong direction. They found a hiding place; tradition says it was a huge hollow log. Before attacking, they carved their identifying marks on several trees so the Sioux would know who had been there. Then, when there was enough light to see, they opened fire on the sleeping Sioux, killing many. They knew it would be suicide to try to take scalps; so they retreated to their hiding place. After the Dakotas were well on the wrong trail, they returned to the village and killed some of the non-fighters left behind, mostly women, children and old men. They then returned to their canoe at St. Anthony Falls and sped home, having fully avenged the humiliation suffered by Chief Curly Head. So much for the truce!

The Branch returned to the south shore of Lake Superior. He married a chief's daughter, whose dowry was a large piece of land on the lake. We know The Branch returned to Gull Lake from time to time and

*A predecessor of the Little Crow of the 1862 Sioux uprising.

on one occasion witnessed the marriage of his daughter to Enmegahbowh (John Johnson) the lay leader of the St. Columba Episcopal Mission.

Chief Curly Head's last official act as principal chief of the Central Minnesota Ojibwe was to attend the Prairie du Chein Conference of 1825, wherein the United States Government brought together representatives of the Ojibwe and Dakota peoples of what is now Minnesota in the hope of ending the more than 100 years of conflict between them. A treaty was negotiated in which the Ojibwe were given not only the Minnesota woodlands but also a large piece of prairie land formerly occupied by the Sioux, extending approximately from the Crow Wing River south to the Watab River. A line was drawn to separate the tribes from what is now Eau Clair, Wisconsin, to the Mississippi River near present day St. Cloud and then continuing west to the Red River. Stakes were planted to mark the boundary.

A very young Hole-in-the-Day was chosen by Curly Head to speak for the Pillagers. He was already an eloquent and creative orator. The Dakota Sioux, naturally, did not want to give up the land in question, and when they were asked by the government representatives what was the basis for their claim, they replied that it had belonged to them and their ancestors for hundreds of years. When Hole-in-the-Day was asked by what right the Pillagers staked their claim, he replied it was by the same right the European Whites had claimed most of the country – by force! The government representatives were hard pressed to refute the Pillager claim!

Curly Head signed the treaty in behalf of his people.

Two tragedies followed: (1) the line was ignored, stakes were pulled and the conflict continued, and (2) Chief Curly Head died of a communicable disease, apparently caught at the conference. He never reached home. Many others of both tribes also died. The illness is not known; there has been speculation it may have been typhoid.

Both of his protégés (his pipe bearers), Song-a-cumig or Strong Ground and Pugona-geshig or Hole-in-the-Day were with him at the time of his death. Tradition has it that before he died, he named Hole-in-the-Day Civil (or administrative) Chief and Strong Ground War Chief of his domain. Curly Head had no children.

Because there were so few Whites in the area in the early 1800s, we know relatively little about Curly Head, as compared to the Hole-in-the-Days, but we do know he had a tremendous impact on the early history of Central Minnesota. Perhaps his greatest contribution was securing the area against the Dakota Sioux, making it much easier for traders, loggers and settlers to enter the area later in the century.

Curly Head was the first Ojibwe leader to make his mark in our area of study. He was the first principal chief (as recognized by the United States Government) of the Gull Lake – Crow Wing – Mississippi band of the Pillager Ojibwe.

We have no photographs or painting or eyewitness accounts of why the chief had such an unusual name, but it is likely that his hair was indeed curly and this would set him apart from other Indians. (Who knows, he may have had some Viking blood?)

CHAPTER III
Chief Hole-In-The-Day the elder
(Pugona-geshig)

As we learned in the last chapter, Chief Curly Head, before he died, named young Hole-in-the-Day (Pugona-geshig) as his successor and the older brother, Strong Ground (Song-a-cumig) as war chief. At the time, Hole-in-the-Day was about twenty-five years of age, and Strong Ground was two or three years older. It was customary for Ojibwe chiefs to pass their title on to their oldest son, but Curly Head was childless. Thus, it is not surprising that he chose one of his pipe bearers as his replacement as Head (or Civil) Chief and the other as War Chief for his people. Curly Head had been both Civil and War Chief.

It was no small honor to be a pipe bearer. An Indian's pipe was his prize possession. For example, when a Red Lake Chief, He-That-is-Spoken-To, arrived at Leech Lake for a conference with Zebulon Pike and discovered he had left the stem of his pipe home, he refused to participate until it had been retrieved. To be a pipe bearer was an apprenticeship to higher rank. These individuals did far more than carry the pipe; they were personal assistants to the chief.

The civil or administrative chief was considered to be the Head Chief and of higher rank than the War Chief. One has to wonder how the older brother, Strong Ground, felt about his "kid brother" out-ranking him. In the years that followed, the brothers remained close and were allies in numerous ventures. Strong Ground later became Head Chief of a large village at the mouth of Pine River.

No doubt there were older men in Curly Head's village that may not have found it easy taking orders from a twenty-five year old, but as we shall see, Hole-in-the-Day was no ordinary person; he was a dynamic, brave, charismatic leader. As noted in the last chapter, Curly Head made him spokesman for the Central Minnesota Pillagers at the Prairie du Chein Conference.

We don't know when the United States Government recognized Hole-in-the-Day as "Principal Chief" of the whole area, but he was of that rank when he signed the Treaty of 1837.

Now that we have jumped ahead and told the story of how he became chief in 1825, let us go back to the birth and formative years of this extraordinary man. Hole-in-the-Day was born, approximately, in 1800 at La Pointe (Madeline Island, Lake Superior, Wisconsin); his brother, Strong Ground, two or three years earlier. Because of the formers unusual name, it has long been assumed that his birth was somehow associated with a solar eclipse. Scientist-historian Carl Zapffe took the time and effort to check the solar records of the span of time during which the chief could possibly have been born. He found no record of an eclipse in this part of the world!

The second possibility, one to which this author subscribes, is that at the moment of birth, the sky was cloudy and suddenly a blue patch appeared; perhaps even the sun was shining through – hence, a hole in the day. There is one other bit of evidence, in the pictorial presentation of the name, there is a circle above the head; it is blank (white). If there had been an association with an eclipse, shouldn't the circle have been filled in (black)?

There was another "Chief Hole-in-the-Day" who lived later on Leech Lake. He was the focal point of the last White-Indian war in 1898, So far as we know, he was not a relative of the Gull Lake Hole-in-the-Days.

As mentioned above, Hole-in-the-Day's family was associated with the south shore of Lake Superior. His brother, Strong Ground, on the other hand, as mentioned in the last chapter, at the age of 10 tagged along with Curly Head and Chief Flat Mouth (of Leech Lake) when they wrecked vengeance on the Dakota Sioux village on the Long Prairie River. As you recall, he hid in the bushes and then rushed out to finish off and scalp a wounded Dakota warrior. So – what was a ten year old from the south shore of Lake Superior doing on Gull Lake? Surely he was with his family. It is fair to conclude that the brothers either spent their childhood here or else the family was living here, or at least visiting here for a time. Hole-in-the-Day's family and Curly Head were of the same totem (crane); they could have been related.

The next we hear about Hole-in-the-Day was when he had reached the age of sixteen, and he thought it was time to choose a wife. Apparently, even at that young age, he was well respected because a powerful chief of the La Pointe Peninsula on the south shore of Lake Superior, Chief White Crane, agreed to let him marry one of his daughters. Earlier, La Pointe had been the capital of the Ojibwe Nation, so White Crane was an important chief.

Hole-in-the-Day finished his teen years at La Pointe.

We next hear of Hole-in-the-Day and his brother as members of the Cass Expedition of 1820. It was as members of this historic venture that the brothers returned to Central Minnesota, and then became pipe bearers to Chief Curly Head.

Before discussing Hole-in-the-Day's remarkable achievement as a member of this expedition, it is appropriate to take a moment to talk about another great man who was its leader, Lewis B. Cass, Governor of Michigan Territory (which then included Minnesota), and later, Democratic candidate for President of the United States.

Lewis Cass served 18 years as governor of the Michigan Territory (which for awhile included Minnesota) and then went on to be Secretary of War (1831-36), Ambassador to France (1836-42), U.S. Senator from the new state of Michigan, Secretary of State under President Buchanan and then three times sought the Democratic nomination for president. On the third try he was successful in winning the endorsement but lost to Zachary Taylor. In Minnesota, Cass Lake and Cass County are named for him.

It was Governor Cass who brought the famous brothers, Song-a-cumig or Strong Ground and Pugona-geshig or Hole-in-the-Day I back to central Minnesota. It should be noted that Henry Schoolcraft, who discovered the source of the Mississippi on a later trip, was also a member of the Cass party.

Lewis B. Cass (1782-1866). Governor of Michigan Territory and Democratic candidate for president.

Courtesy, Chicago Historical Society

Hole-in-the-Day joined the expedition at Mackinac. It is amazing how well traveled Indians were in that day. The young brave was visiting traders there and became enthralled with the idea of joining Cass as he journeyed first to the Ojibwe country of what is now Minnesota and then down the Mississippi into Sioux territory. The purposes of the expedition was to learn more about the huge Michigan Territory and to make sure everyone therein knew it was now part of the United States. Hole-in-the-Day persuaded the local traders to recommend him to Cass and he was accepted. It is possible that Strong Ground was there, but he many have joined the party later when it reached Lake Superior where the brothers' village was located. We know he was with the Cass expedition when it was in what is now Minnesota.

When the expedition reached Sault Ste. Marie, Hole-in-the-Day proved to be a great asset to Governor Cass. The Indians there were loyal to the British and threatened to massacre the Cass party which had only 65 members.

By the time the very delicate situation was resolved, it was estimated that over 2000 hostile Ojibwe were threatening to annihilate the Cass party. One chief, Sassaba, went so far as to raise a British Flag outside his tent, which was on U.S. soil. Cass, in a dramatic display of bravery, marched into the Indian village with only an interpreter at his side. He tore down the Union Jack and trampled it in the mud and then broke the staff over his knee. He then shouted, "If you ever dare insult the United States of America in this manner again, we will fire on you."

In fairness to the Ojibwe, we should acknowledge that they had been British subjects for many years and did not fully understand that after the War of 1812 this was American territory. One of the major purposes of the Cass expedition was to make it clear that all of the Michigan Territory was now a part of the United States.

C.C. Trowbridge, who was a member of the expedition, and who kept a journal reported, "In less than ten minutes every woman and child with all their baggage was on the opposite side of the river. The Indians prepared themselves, expecting an attack from us, and we being under the same apprehension from them, loaded our arms, doubled our guard, and made every preparation to sell our lives as dearly as possible."

At this point, Chief Ke-wakwish-kum of the Grand Rapids (Michigan) Ojibwe, who were a part of the Cass expedition, recognized the odds and announced to the Governor that he and his men simply could not fire on members of their own tribe. The chief and his men threw down their guns.

It was then that Hole-in-the-Day, only twenty years of age, stepped forward to the exact spot where Ke-wakwish-kum had addressed the governor and gave a short, but spellbinding speech that marked him as a truly great leader. It is unfortunate that we have no pictures of Hole-in-the-Day, but his contemporaries characterized him as being tall, a remarkable physical specimen and with handsome facial features. Just out of his teens, he must have had a dramatic physical presence as he began: "Father, you were hesitant in accepting me into your party, and only did so because of the urgent recommendation of the traders at Michilimackinac. I now wish to show you why they said what they did. All I ask is that you give me a good rifle." He then fired the rifle into the air to get everyone's attention, and then addressed the Ojibwe, "Nikanissag! (friends) Our white father is right! You all know as well as I that whatever the rights and claims the English may have had on these lands of ours, those rights and claims were won by the Americans in open and fair battle, and not one but on two different occasions.

We judge the outcome of our own battles in exactly the same way. Therefore I can see this White Father in no other light than that which he claims. So if fight we must, I myself shall be found on the side of the White Father, and under his American flag! Any who dare approach his camp as enemies approach as my enemy, and shall pay dearly!

Are any of you with me?"*

An observer reported, "Immediately a hundred more stood by his side, ready to obey his commands, while our hero continued to thunder defiance at those favoring the foreign flag rather than the rightful American flag, and challenging to combat any who dared molest either the White Father or the flag of the Americans. No one dared raise a hand against either him or the Governor."

It was thought by those present that were it not for Hole-in-the-Day, all would have been massacred!

But the tension was not over, and as night fell, no one was certain what morning would bring. Unknown to either Cass or Hole-in-the-Day, George Johnston, son of an Ojibwe mother (Golden Meadow Woman) and a white man (his father was also called George Johnston), called a meeting across the river of the Ojibwe chiefs and helped persuade them to accept the fact this was now American soil and to allow the Cass Expedition to go on its way.

Trowbridge wrote in his diary, "Day broke and we all found ourselves wearing our scalps".

Governor Cass recognized Hole-in-the-Day's great contribution to the continuation and success of his mission by asking him to gather the Ojibwe. He then addressed him thus, "Through the authority invested in me, Sir, by our Great White Father in Washington, I hereby designate you a chief, now and forever after in the eyes of every American. With you, we shall hereafter deal directly, as the chief of your own band of these faithful and dedicated warriors, and of all others of any band who may subsequently choose to join you."

Governor Cass then gave Hole-in-the-Day a Presidential medal and told him he could keep the rifle he had borrowed. He also gave him an American flag.

Trowbridge remembered the dramatic experience this way:

During this part of the scene our attention and admiration were particularly attracted by the conduct of one of our Indians, a young man of a very uncommonly prepossessing appearance and dignified deportment for a native, who – when the other Indians of our party strongly protested against taking arms at opposition to their brethren – came to the Governor and demanded a gun with ammunition etc., saying that the conduct of the others should be no rule for his conduct, and that as he had joined the Governor's party with the expectation of sharing the difficulties and dangers with them, he would now, however repugnant to his feelings, offer his services against his relatives and acquaintances in the same manner as if they were his enemies. For from what he had observed, he consid-

This quotation is taken from Carl Zapffe's book, "Indian Days" and is what Zapffe imagined Hole-in-the-Day said, based on comments made later by those present.

ered their conduct highly reprehensible.

Strong Ground is not mentioned as being present on this occasion, but he did join the Cass Expedition at some point, because Cass did present him with a medal and he was a member of the group as they proceeded across Minnesota. Hole-in-the-Day continued with Cass to the end of his journey, but then both he and Strong Ground reappeared at Gull Lake. It was then when Curly Head commissioned them as pipe bearers.

As mentioned in the last chapter, there was a third and younger brother, Zhe-gud (or The Branch) who joined the two older brothers in Curly Head's village for a couple of years but returned to Sault Ste. Marie with his family in 1822. But during those two years the three brothers, entirely on their own, attacked Sioux villages at least twice. These adventures of course added to their fame. Apparently The Branch (Zhe-gud) remained in contact with the Gull Lake village because his daughter, years later, married John Johnson (En-me-gah-bowh), the deacon at the St. Columba Mission. This is particularly interesting in that Hole-in-the-Day II had a strong dislike for Johnson and often threatened to kill him; yet, Johnson was married to his cousin.

In the late 1820's, Hole-in-the-Day was recognized as "Second Chief" of the Sandy Lake village, which was then the capital of the Ojibwe nation. Apparently he had authority in both villages at the same time. The Principal Chief at Sandy Lake was Ka ta wa be day* and Hole-in-the-Day married his daughter, taking her as his second wife. Kwi wi sens, or Hole-in-the-Day II, was their first child.

John Smith the hero of Carl Zapffe's book, "The Man Who Lived in Three Centuries," told of an interesting experience he had with Hole-in-the-Day I after he had become the Head Chief. It seems Hole-in-the-Day's medicine man had a vision of a Sioux village, which could be easily conquered and said that he would lead his chief to the location. Hole-in-the-Day invited Smith to join him. The following is Smith's account of what happened next:

Not forgetting my early pledge to spill the blood of those who had murdered my sister and brother, I consented gladly; and, summoning all the warriors of my then great tribe, we started out upon the warpath. The combined assault was headed by Hole-in-the-Day, though guided by the Medicine Man. Three days passed in transit; and on the morning of the fourth the stage of the stealthy approach began.

Sure enough! Exactly in the position predicted by the Medicine Man, there stood a Dakota village, lying peaceably in a small valley. From one of the lodges issued a thin and lazy column of smoke. Otherwise

*Sometimes spelled "Ka-Tiwabiday." He was the son of Baiaswa, the legendary Ojibwe chief who led the invasion of the Sioux-held Minnesota woodlands from his base in Wisconsin.

there was no noise, neither any signs of life.

Creeping with exceeding precaution, the warriors came within gunshot, and the Chief gave the fatal signal. A simultaneous volley thundered down the little valley, lead balls pouring with well-considered spacing into every one of the teepees. The only answer was the dismal howl of a dog.

Because Smith's sole purpose in agreeing to accompany Hole-in-the-Day was to discover an opportunity for revenging the deaths in his family, he now boldly stepped forward to take the initiative in bringing this battle to its hoped-for climax. Furthermore, deep inside he felt extremely confident

John Smith – The Man Who Lived in Three Centuries; an ally of Hole-in-the-Day I

Courtesy of the Minnesota Historical Society

"that no enemy bullet could kill me, as I hold a charmed life".

Not waiting to reload his gun, and grabbing nothing but his battle-ax, Smith raced to the nearest lodge—the one having a slight issue of smoke. He bounded right through the doorway and with such fierce energy as calculated to take any opponent by surprise. But he found nothing except the dog. The exciting wisps of smoke were issuing from a few lazy embers, apparently remaining from a fire that had been abandoned hours before. Plunging his tomahawk into the body of the unfortunate dog, Smith dashed back outside and ordered his warriors to search the village. All dwellings proved to be empty. Hole-in-the-Day was so intensely angered over this useless enterprise that he immediately killed "Big Medicine Man."

After spending several years at Gull Lake, Hole-in-the-Day moved south to the mouth of the Crow Wing and, later, to the mouth of the Little Elk River, just north of the site of present-day Little Falls. Here he protected the southern frontier of the Ojibwe. At times the pressures from the Sioux were too much and he would be forced to retreat to Whitefish or to Rabbit Lake, which were also a part of his domain.

MORE FIGHTING BETWEEN HOLE-IN-THE-DAY'S WARRIORS AND THE DAKOTA SIOUX

In 1838, Hole-in-the-Day played a major role in a series of bloody

Views of Fort Snelling, Minnesota

Courtesy Minnesota Historical Soc

confrontations between the Dakotas and the Ojibwe. In April of that year, he and a party of nine braves stumbled onto a camp of Sioux on the Chippewa River (a tributary of the Minnesota); they were mostly women and children temporarily separated from a hunting party. Professing peace, they were warmly welcomed and dined on dog meat—one of the Indians' choice delicacies. That night, on signal, Hole-in-the-Day and his men fell on the Sioux and killed all but three.

On August 2, Sioux relatives of the massacre victims had an opportunity for revenge. They surprised Hole-in-the-Day and five companions near Fort Snelling; one of the Indians with whom Hole-in-the-Day had exchanged clothing—or ornaments—was killed and another wounded (both were Ottawa's). When one of the Sioux ran in to collect what he believed to be the scalp of Hole-in-the-Day, White Fisher, who was in the Ojibwe party, shot him. The famous Indian Agent, Taliaferro, came on the scene at that point, and the Sioux fled. The Ojibwe were taken to the fort and the Ottawa Indian was buried there. Hole-in-the-Day was escorted across the river and had to find his way home on his own.

When they heard of the incident, the chiefs of the neighboring Sioux villages came to the fort, as well as the leadership of the Red Wing band of Lake Pepin—to which the young Sioux belonged who had killed the Ottawa.

At the insistence of the commander of the fort, Major Plympton, the two young braves were turned over to him and placed in custody, but the chiefs pleaded for their lives. After being satisfied that the Sioux leadership would properly punish their young warriors, Major Plympton released them to their custody. The punishment administered by the ranking Sioux braves to the culprits was traditional; their blankets, leggings and breechcloths were cut into small pieces; their hair was cut short (signifying great humiliation); and they were heavily flogged. One Ojibwe was dead; one Sioux was dead; the score was even, and it seemed peace would be continued.

However, the following year, 1839, Hole-in-the-Day with five hundred Gull Lake people, another hundred from the Crow Wing area, one hundred fifty from Leech Lake, and another contingent from Mille Lacs Lake all arrived at the St. Peter's Agency (by Fort Snelling) under the mistaken notion that they could collect certain annuities due them. Twelve hundred Sioux arrived at the agency for the same purpose (but under a different treaty). The Ojibwe were told they would have to go to La Pointe to collect what they had coming, but they were given some food. Surprisingly enough, the historic enemies got along well and even danced and played games together. After a month, the food ran out and the Ojibwe began their return journeys to the north. Two of Hole-in-the-Day's men who were related to the warrior shot the previous year stopped at the fort to weep over the grave of their slain kinsman. Inspired to seek revenge, they approached the Lake Calhoun camp of the Dakotas at night—some think with the knowledge and encouragement of Hole-in-the-Day. At daybreak they killed a departing hunter named Nika. The slain Sioux turned out to be a highly respected warrior, brother-in-law of the chief, and nephew of the famous medicine man, Red Bird.

Revenge came quickly. One contingent of about one hundred warriors—under Little Crow (a predecessor of the Little Crow who led the Sioux uprising in 1862)—surprised a large band of Ojibwe near the present site of Stillwater. They were finally driven off but not before killing twenty-one and wounding twenty-nine Ojibwe. The second contingent, under Red Bird, pursued the Mille Lacs Lake band. Before leaving, the pipe of war was passed down the rows of Sioux warriors and Red Bird followed, laying hands on the heads of each and swearing them to strike without pity, taking no captives. After locating the Mille Lacs Indians, they waited until most braves had gone on ahead to hunt. The old men, women and children left behind were at first easy prey, but the hunters returned quickly and a bitter struggle ensued. The Sioux took seventy scalps but lost seventeen braves of their own, including Red Bird and his son. The Ojibwe scalps were hung from their lodge poles at Lake Calhoun and the celebrating went on for a month.

Major Lawrence Taliaferro, the Indian agent who founded Eatonville on Lake Calhoun, Minneapolis.

Courtesy: Library of Congress

Taliaferro was keenly disappointed and left the agency soon thereafter. He had taken a special interest and pride in the Lake Calhoun settlement where he had been quite successful in encouraging agricultural practices. He had given the settlement the name "Eatonville." And so the bloody conflict between the two tribes continued for another generation.

TREATY OF 1837*

Chief Hole-in-the-Day I and his brother, Strong Ground, were among

---

* The entire Treaty of 1837 is reproduced in the appendix.

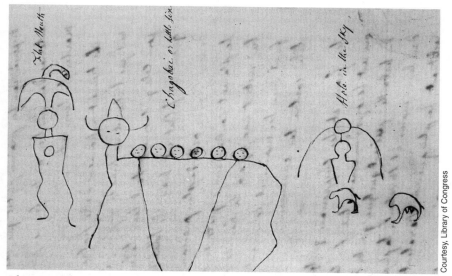

The pictorial signatures of three powerful Minnesota Chiefs: Flat Mouth, Shakopee, and Hole-in-the-Day I.

the chiefs who signed this treaty with the U.S. Government. Although it ceded a huge area of land to the American government, it was mostly about logging rights. Parts of the Midwest were being settled by Whites and there was a great need for timber to build not only houses, but also schools, churches, factories etc. The pine and hardwood timber of the woodlands north of St. Paul were the most easily accessed at that time. As seen on the map on page 48, it was an inverted triangle between the St. Croix and Mississippi Rivers. It included Mille Lacs Lake. The infant village of Crow Wing was at the northwest tip of the triangle. This, then, was the first land logged in what is not the State of Minnesota.

The treaty promised the Ojibwe, annually, for a term of twenty years, the following payments:

Nine thousand five hundred dollars to be paid in money.
Nineteen thousand dollars to be delivered in goods.
Three thousand dollars for establishing three blacksmith shops.
One thousand dollars for farmers (mostly for seed).
Two thousand dollars in provisions.
Five hundred dollars in tobacco.

In these early treaties, much of the money went to individual chiefs; usually it was paid in gold. There were often questions raised about both

TREATIES BETWEEN MINNESOTA INDIAN TRIBES
AND THE UNITED STATES GOVERNMENT[1]

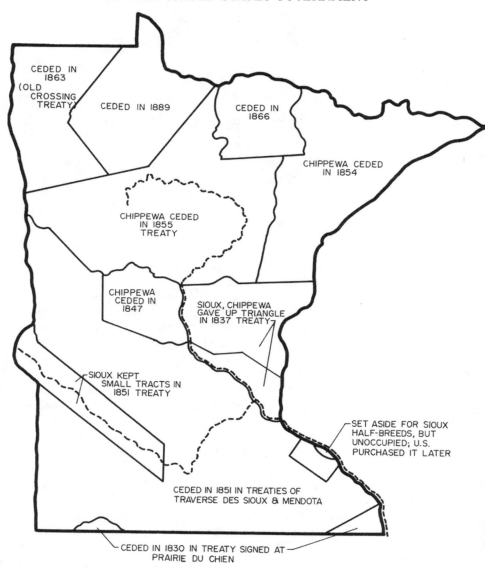

CEDED IN 1863 (OLD CROSSING TREATY)

CEDED IN 1889

CEDED IN 1866

CHIPPEWA CEDED IN 1854

CHIPPEWA CEDED IN 1855 TREATY

CHIPPEWA CEDED IN 1847

SIOUX, CHIPPEWA GAVE UP TRIANGLE IN 1837 TREATY

SIOUX KEPT SMALL TRACTS IN 1851 TREATY

SET ASIDE FOR SIOUX HALF-BREEDS, BUT UNOCCUPIED; U.S. PURCHASED IT LATER

CEDED IN 1851 IN TREATIES OF TRAVERSE DES SIOUX & MENDOTA

CEDED IN 1830 IN TREATY SIGNED AT PRAIRIE DU CHIEN

[1]*Red Lake Reserve not shown*

Hole-in-the-Days as to how much filtered down to the lesser chiefs and other members of the tribe, and how much they may have kept for themselves.

The Treaty of 1837 has been very much in the news in recent years because the Ojibwe were promised hunting and fishing privileges indefinitely unless revoked by the President of the United States. The Ojibwe of the area started exercising these rights again in the 1990s. Those opposed to the claim have pointed out that President Taylor did revoke the hunting and fishing privileges. The Ojibwe claimed that in subsequent administrations the rights were reinstated, although not by a president directly. Therein lay the controversy and it went all the way to the U.S. Supreme Court where the Ojibwe were the winners by a majority of one vote (1999). The controversy probably is not over.

HOLE-IN-THE-DAY I DIES YOUNG

Chief Hole-in-the-Day I died in 1847 at an age of about forty-six years. He was returning from Pig's Eye (St. Paul) where he had been drinking and was being carried home on the floor of a wagon. As the entourage was crossing the Platte River he fell from the wagon and was critically injured. His warriors carried him to a nearby home; here he regained consciousness long enough to pass on the mantle of authority and a few words of wisdom to his son – Kwi-wi-sens (or "Boy"). When he died, he was buried according to his instructions on Baldur Bluff, (just north of Little Falls) – overlooking the Mississippi. Here, in death, he continued his vigil for the canoes of the Sioux.

It should be noted that by some other accounts Hole-in-the-Day drowned when the wagon fell into the Platte River.

Hole-in-the-Day was described by the white men who knew him as tall, handsome and athletic. He was a charismatic leader of his people, an orator and a brave warrior. Both he and his son, Hole-in-the-Day the Younger, may be thought of as scoundrels by the standards of today's culture, but when judged by the culture of

1847
BURIAL MOUND OF
CHIEF HOLE-IN-THE-DAY
DONATED BY THE
LITTLE FALLS GRANITE WORKS

The grave marker of Chief Hole-in-the-Day the Elder on Baldur's Bluff just north of Little Falls, overlooking the Mississippi River.

Photo credit: "The Man Who Lived in Three Centuries", Carl Zapffe.

their time, they must be characterized as outstanding leaders of their people.

As for Hole-in-the-Day's older brother, Strong Ground, we know that in addition to being war chief for the Crow Wing – Gull Lake – Mississippi Pillager Ojibwes, he was civil chief of a fairly large village of his own on Pine River. It is said that when he died (so far as we know of natural causes) he was eligible to wear 38 feathers in his headdress, one for each Sioux warrior he had slain.

CHAPTER IV
Chief Hole-In-The-Day the younger
(Kwi-wi-sens or Boy)

His real name was "Boy", but when he signed the Treaty of 1847, shortly after his father's death, the representatives of the U.S. Government identified his "X" as Hole-in-the-Day, and that became his official name even though other Ojibwe sometimes still called him Kwi-Wi-Sens, or Boy. But as the son of a principal chief and grandson of another (Ka ta wa be day of Sandy Lake), Hole-in-the-Day the Younger was a true hereditary Chief. His great grandfather was Baias-wa, who led the Ojibwe invasion in 1766.

In Ojibwe tradition, as stated in the last chapter, the position of chief was usually inherited; thus it was appropriate for Hole-in-the-Day, the elder, to pass his title on to his son. Otherwise, if there were no son or the son was too young or did not perform adequately, lesser chiefs (and sometimes the other men of the tribe) would agree on who should be the leading chief. As indicated earlier, the American Government labeled that person "Principal Chief" and that individual was invited to sign all treaties and be spokesman for his people. In modern times, American Indian tribes generally elect their chief executive – many of whom are now women.

In general, American Indians still believe their leaders should be:
• charismatic
• skilled at something
• persuasive and
• spiritual in nature.

Chief Hole-in-the-Day II inherited his title at the tender age of nineteen or twenty; one has to wonder how long it took before his leadership was fully accepted by the older sub-chiefs and the other Ojibwe of the area.

The U.S. Government arbitrarily decided who were to be the principal chiefs, but they made these decisions after consultation with traders and sometimes missionaries as to whom the tribe and other chiefs accepted as the leading chief. Because of his youth, it is hard to imag-

ine that Hole-in-the-Day was not challenged, and we do know that he and his neighbor on Gull Lake, Chief Bad Boy, did not get along and when the Sandy Lake Reservation headquarters was moved to Gull River in 1855 and Hole-in-the-Day was selected by the government to sign that treaty, Bad Boy moved his village to Mille Lacs Lake. Of course, the fact Hole-in-the-Day had threatened to kill him may also have been a consideration!

The relationship between Hole-in-the-Day and Bad Boy had further deteriorated when three of the former's young men murdered a white peddler on the shore of Round Lake* and Bad Boy's men captured the culprits and turned them over to the sheriff at Little Falls. A posse of Whites relieved the sheriff of the young braves while on their way to Fort Snelling. They hung them, chained and handcuffed together, near the mouth of the Little Elk River and buried them—still handcuffed together.

The younger Hole-in-the-Day, however, had a lot going for him. He had inherited his father's stature and good looks and also had comparable oratorical skills. He also had a great deal of self-confidence, bordering on arrogance, and was not afraid to lead. Also because treaty payments (not individual allotments) were paid to him, he had plenty of economic clout.

Hole-in-the-Day II was the last of the great Ojibwe Chiefs.

That is not to say that great Ojibwe leadership has not followed, but after Hole-in-the-Day the power base was gone. Indian lands had been signed away in treaty after treaty and the rout of the Sioux in 1862 left white man clearly in control of Minnesota and the destiny of the American Indian.

Hole-in-the-Day had several houses and pieces of property. He had headquarters at both Crow Wing and Gull Lake. It is believed that the log cabin located at Highway 371 and the Mission Road was his (later, Chief Wadena's). He built a cabin several hundred yards east of his father's earlier home in Ojibwe Park—between Round and Long Lakes.

Hole-in-the-Day also had a farm, of which he was very proud, on the Gull River, near where it leaves the lake.

Old Hole-in-the-Day had raised "Boy" to be tough, hard, and aggressive. When a lad not yet in his teens (1838), his father "arranged" for him to stab and scalp a Sioux girl of about the same age.

Photo at Left: Chief Hole-in-the-Day the Younger. As was his custom in posing for pictures, he was dressed partly in whiteman's garb and partly in Ojibwe. This picture is thought to have been taken in the early 1850s. The three medals may include one given his father by Governor Cass. He is holding a traditional warclub.

Photo Courtesy of Crow Wing County Historical Society.

Some other buildings owned by White settlers were also burned at this time.

Hole-in-the-Day II got the attention of Territorial Governor Ramsey and most Minnesotans in 1850 when he and a small party (perhaps only one or two others) attacked six Sioux (taking one scalp) just across the river from St. Paul (after hiding in the gorge of Fountain Cave). The attack was probably in reprisal for the Sioux annihilation of a party of fifteen Ojibwe a little more than a month earlier on the Apple River in Wisconsin. Governor Ramsey summoned the chiefs of both the Sioux and the Ojibwe to a peace council at Fort Snelling. On June 9th, Hole-in-the-Day arrived with about 100 braves; later the following morning about 300 Sioux arrived on horseback; they dismounted in a display of pageantry and saluted the Ojibwe who had lined up to welcome them. Governor Ramsey presided personally at the council. William Warren, the Ojibwe historian and resident of Old Crow Wing whom we have quoted earlier, read the charges against the Sioux, and Bad Hail read the counter-charges against the Ojibwe. All sides finally agreed to abide by the provisions of the treaty of 1843 and the council concluded with a feast.

Earlier in the proceedings the Sioux Chiefs had left the council in protest of the presence of some white women who were on hand as members of the Governor's party. Hole-in-the-Day II scored a coup by offering the women seats among his people. However, the women thought it best to leave, and when the Sioux returned they were sharply taken to task by Governor Ramsey. But the council concluded peacefully and to the satisfaction of the Governor, but mistrust on both sides was still evident as hostages were required to insure safe journeys home.

THE CIVIL WAR AND INDIAN RECRUITMENT

Attempts were made to draw the Minnesota Ojibwe into the Civil War on the side of the North. John Johnson whose Indian name was Enmegahbowh (the one who stands before his people), as mentioned earlier, served as a deacon of the Episcopal Mission (St. Columba) on Gull Lake. He reported that a man named Horn, a whiskey trader, tried to recruit Ojibwe warriors for Fort Snelling, where whey would become Union soldiers. Johnson said that he was asked by Horn to help him recruit braves from Mille Lacs Lake; he refused. Horn reportedly paid between fifty and two hundred dollars as a "signing bonus" – which in most cases was spent on Horn's whiskey before the braves reached the fort.

Fathers of some of the Leech Lake warriors who had been recruited were so upset they came to Gull Lake looking for Horn with the intent to kill him. Johnson persuaded the fathers to hold off while he made a trip to Fort Snelling to try to stop the practice. He approached Henry

Rice and Commandant Henry Sibley. The latter said he was unaware of the practice and promised to put a stop to it. When Johnson reported this back to the fathers, they were satisfied and returned to Leech Lake.

DAKOTA SIOUX AND OJIBWE UPRISINGS IN 1862

When the civil war broke out, the American Indian was anxious, puzzled, and tempted. He had seen white man's governments topple before. The British had replaced the French and the American "Long Knives" had replaced the British and in 1812 the British had threatened to reclaim their lost ground. Was the Great White Father in Washington on the way out? White civilization had not given the Indian much cause to rejoice; if there would ever be an opportunity to reclaim his old lands and rid the area of the white man—it was then.

The Minnesota Sioux seemed less fearful of white man as a result of the Civil War. The Ojibwe were not so sure, but Hole-in-the-Day II was apparently ready to take a chance. Historians do not agree whether or not there was collaboration between these age-old rival tribes, but there is evidence that Chiefs Little Crow and Hole-in-the-Day II conspired while they were together at Fort Snelling.

Chief Little Crow in 1858—general of the great Sioux uprising in 1862.

In his letters to Nathan Richardson of Little Falls, John Johnson (Enmegahbowh) stated that Hole-in-the-Day had received a message from Little Crow, which invited the Ojibwe to join the fight against the Whites.

At any rate, both tribes went on the offense on the very same day, on August 18, 1862, when the Sioux and the Ojibwe swung into action more than one hundred miles apart. The simultaneous attacks were supposedly timed for the middle day of the three-day dark of the moon period, which occurs monthly—when there is no moon at all, all night long. Hole-in-the-Day attacked St. Columba Mission and the Lutheran Church on Mission Lake and Little Crow attacked the white settlers in the New Ulm area. It is hard to believe it was coincidental.

There was at least one important difference in the two attacks—Little Crow had the support of the vast majority of his people; Hole-in-the-

Day controlled only the Gull Lake-Crow Wing area. He had been in communication, however, with the Ojibwe at Leech Lake, Battle Lake, Ottertail and elsewhere and thought he could count on their support. If he had been correct in his assumption, northern Minnesota could have been subjected to the same bloodbath as the Minnesota River Valley. As it was, southern Minnesota became the setting for the most devastating massacre in the nation's history. This atrocity, plus the annihilation of Custer and his men at Little Big Horn and the culmination of Whiteman's reprisals at Wounded Knee, taken together, are the most deplorable chapter in the history of white-Indian relations.

As with all wars, there were direct causes or incidents, which triggered the fighting and then the more significant indirect causes. Let us examine the latter, first. The Indians had many reasons for dissatisfaction and concern: (1) there was an obvious westward movement of Whites with a ravenous hunger for land: (2) Indian policies of the United States Government were disheartening—treaty payments were late and meager. Indian Agents were political appointees, often ill prepared for their jobs, and the Indians were literally compressed into reservations; and (3) the very nature of the Sioux people, at least at that time, was warlike and aggressive and they were not accustomed to being pushed around without fighting back.

The incident that triggered this war was the killing of five whites by four Wahpeton braves on the farm of Howard Baker near Acton. Understanding the significance of the murders, the Sioux debated long into the night what course of action to take. Tradition holds that Little Crow opposed further violence against the Whites, comparing the white soldiers who would come for revenge to "clouds of grasshoppers".

Some believe that Little Crow yielded to his hot-blooded braves in fear that they would turn elsewhere for leadership. They had already turned not long before to another chief called "Traveling Hail" for "chief speaker." And so the die was cast and the balance of the night was spent in preparation for attack. The next day, August 18, 1862, Little Crow lead about two hundred warriors against the Redwood Indian Agency. Victory came easily.

Now, if indeed there was collusion between Hole-in-the-Day and Little Crow and the date of the uprising was pre-set, then some of the above version of how the action started is in doubt.

There is every evidence that the Whites of Minnesota were completely surprised by the uprising. Frontier newspapers of the day gave no indication of immediate concern, even though it was common knowledge that the treaty payments due the Indians were long overdue.

Sioux victories came quickly following the success at the Lower Agency; (1) of forty-six soldiers who followed Captain John Marsh out of

Execution of the thirty-eight Sioux Indians at Mankato Minnesota December 26, 1862.

Courtesy Library of Congress

Fort Ridgley on their way to Redwood, more than half; including the captain, perished; (2) more than fifty members of German farm families in Brown and Nicollet Counties were also killed on the first day; (3) New Ulm was attacked twice – but survived; (4) more than eight hundred Sioux lay siege to Fort Ridgley – but the fort held; and (5) at the ambush at Birch Coulee, more than eighty soldiers were killed. Estimates ran as high as five hundred Whites killed and a thousand wounded; the number of Indian casualties remains unknown. But in a matter of weeks it was all over.

Sibley amassed an army of more than 1600 men; many more were in reserve. Sheer numbers made it just a matter of time until the Sioux would have to accept the futility of their uprising. The Battle of Wood Lake was fought on September 23. Although a massive action, only seven soldiers were killed or died later as a result. There was a futile Sioux attack on Fort Abercrombie a few days later, followed by isolated skirmishes, but the war was over. Little Crow and his surviving warriors fled to the Dakotas and Canada. The Battle of Little Big Horn and the tragedy of Wounded Knee were yet to come, along with dozens of smaller skirmishes, but for Minnesotans there would be only one more armed clash between Whites and Indians – and that would be at Leech Lake thirty-six years later.

As an aftermath to the war, more than 300 Sioux prisoners were condemned to death. Because of the huge number, Sibley decided to share the burden of decision by referring the final judgment to General Pope. The general, in turn, passed it on to that desk "where the buck always stops"—to President Lincoln, himself. Even though already heavily

Courtesy of the Crow Wing County Historical Society

St. Columba Indian Mission of Gull Lake, sketched in 1852. It was Hole-in-the-Day's first target.

burdened by the great Civil War, President Lincoln ordered a review of each case, individually, and expressed his desire that no man should die merely because he participated in the war. Only those who had murdered civilians or were guilty of rape (just two cases) were to pay with their lives. It is said that in the end, Lincoln personally reviewed the history of each man he sentenced to death. On his written order, thirty-eight Sioux warriors were hanged, simultaneously, in Mankato on December 26, 1862.

Following the uprising a $500 price was placed on Little Crow's head and the state paid bounties for Sioux scalps. Little Crow returned to Minnesota with a few braves and was killed by a hunting party near Hutchinson. The reward was collected by Nathan Lawson. Little Crow's body was identified by his deformed hands and wrists, the result of a quarrel with his brothers over who would become chief following the death of his father. He became the third "Little Crow" of his tribe. When the bullet had passed through his wrists, he had gone to Fort Snelling for help. The surgeon suggested amputation, Little Crow decided to gamble and with the help of his own medicine man and "mother nature", he was able to use his hands. He was killed on July 3, 1863. The next day his body was dragged through the streets of Hutchinson as part of the July 4th celebration and finally cast on the city dump. Later he was buried in St. Paul. More than 100 years later he was re-buried by the Big Sioux River near Flandreau, South Dakota.

The much smaller settlements of Mdewakanton Sioux* near present day Shakopee and Prairie Island did not participate in the conflict and were allowed to stay in Minnesota.

As we have said earlier, as Little Crow was leading the Dakotas against the Redwood Agency, Hole-in-the-Day II was at the very same time directing the obliteration of the St. Columba Episcopal Mission on Gull Lake and the burning of a Lutheran mission on Lower Mission Lake. The latter mission was located where a creek leaves the lake and runs to the Mississippi.

So, why did Hole-in-the-Day choose these two little churches as the victims of his first attack when he could have chosen the Indian agency or the Village of Crow Wing? Probably because they were easy prey and he was waiting for reinforcements from Leech Lake and other Ojibwe villages. If there was collaboration between Hole-in-the-Day and Little Crow, then he knew he had to do something dramatic on the agreed day but he did not want to risk defeat with reinforcements on the way.

The burning of the churches was a cheap victory. In the case of the Gull Lake church, the white clergy had been frightened away five years earlier in 1857 and had left it in the care of Enmegahbowh. The faithful Ottawa Indian and his family had been warned and had taken flight by canoe to Crow Wing and then Fort Ripley the night before the attack.

Flush with the satisfaction from the successful completion of his acts of defiance, the chief was now ready for a more ambitious attack on the agency or Crow Wing or, eventually, Fort Ripley. But the leadership of the Leech Lake bands were having second thoughts. The younger warriors had quickly captured the Whites in the area, actually, only seven, and proposed a public execution. However, two respected chiefs, Buffalo and Big Dog, were not so sure Hole-in-the-Day II would be the eventual victor. Wisely they persuaded their braves to bring the captives to Gull Lake, reasoning that if Hole-in-the-Day had changed his mind or had not been successful, the Leech Lake Indians would be left alone to feel the wrath of the Whites. After a two-day journey, they arrived at the appointed rendezvous between Round Lake and Gull Lake. At one point, just prior to the burning of the mission, Hole-in-the-Day decided to attack the Indian Agency; located on the Gull River where it enters the Crow Wing.

John Johnson (Enmegahabowh) in his letters to Nathan Richardson, (a Little Falls judge and history buff) describes what happened:

I stayed at Gull Lake Mission. All the white missionaries had deserted me and had gone to the congenial country for their coward

---

*The Mdewakanton originally lived on Mille Lacs Lake but vacated that area during the Ojibwe invasion.

Courtesy of the Minnesota Historical Society

Chiefs Big Dog, on the left, and Buffalo of Leech Lake. They ended up opposing Hole-in-the-Day's battle plans.

spirits. I understood that the warriors were proposing to attack the Agency. When I heard this, I yoked up my horned horses to flee away to Crow Wing. I started in the early part of the night. When I had gone about half way, in the morning, four warriors overtook us and said I must return home, and that no harm would be done us. Here I was with my wife and children undecided what course to take. My wife advised me to return home. When we arrived home Hole-in-the-Day came to see us and said that we must not be alarmed, and that no harm would be done us.

In the course of a few days, Chief Crossing Sky of Rabbit Lake came to my house in the darkest hour of the night, and said, "I am come to advise you to prepare to flee away to Fort Ripley. Hole-in-the-Day is going to march with his warriors to the Agency in two days from today and massacre all the whites. Be sure to flee away. For when he returns he will be so ugly and spare no one whom he knows has sympathy with the whites."

The chief went out. My wife cried, and said, "The people, then, must be informed what is coming upon them. If I cannot find any-one to bear the news I will go. There is no time to lose."

The time was short; but it so happened that a white man came in late in the evening to ask me what was the meaning of so much drumming and so many war whoops. I told him all about it, and

Enmegahbowh (The Rev. John Johnson), an Ottawa Indian, custodian of St. Columba Mission and later ordained an Episcopal clergyman. His Indian name translates "He who stands before his people".

Judge Nathan Richardson of Little Falls, the man to whom John Johnson (Enmegahbowh) addressed his letters.

urged him to carry my letter to the people of the Agency, that they may be preparing shelter or a strong stockade for their defense. For a long time he would not go. He was very fearful. I said to him, "The Indians will find out you are here with me and will kill you. If you cannot go, my wife will go." At last with much fear he started away with my message. This poor man's name was Yankknight. You must have known him, for he lived at Crow Wing for many years.

Sure enough, one Saturday afternoon Hole-in-the-Day and his warriors passed through near my door, naked and painted black all over his body and singing war songs. My wife cried after the warriors had passed away out of sight. I said to her that I apprehended no danger for the people there, for they must have received my letter and have had plenty of time to prepare them a strong stockade. When they received my letter both the women and children worked like beavers.

Hole-in-the-Day with his warriors arrived at the Agency and halted a quarter of a mile away. It was about morning or before daybreak. He sent two warriors to go and see whether any preparation had been made against being attacked. To their great astonishment they find that an old heavy log house, built by the soldier's years ago, strongly, with heavy logs, was now full of lights, and all around the building were port holes, and each port hole contained two or three guns well loaded.

About a month before this several boxes of guns arrived at the Agency. From the beginning and for many years, the government had given them guns and ammunition with their annual payments. The guns had arrived and the doomed people opened the boxes, and had plenty of ammunition to use to shoot the hearts of the Indians.

The spies returned to bear the message to Hole-in-the-Day and told him that the people were well fortified, and it was of no use to attack them, for "before we can kill one single white squaw, many of us will be shot down and caused to kiss the dust. They have been warned what was coming upon them."

Hole-in-the-Day jumped up with vengeance of exasperation and said "Let us return home. I know the treacherous man who gave the information. Enmegahbowh is the man. He shall surely die and just as soon as we reach home. The first thing I shall do is go to his house and shoot him down like a dog. Mark you" said he to his warriors, "all of you shall see me doing it, and shall bear witness to the act."

At this time I was safely housed and protected in the hands of the government soldiers. Sure enough when Hole-in-the-Day and his party arrived at home and came opposite my house he halted and with his loaded gun started to go to my house. He found that I had gone to some place. He said again, "He must die. I shall not let him go. I shall find him where he has fled.

Until his death, Hole-in-the-Day continued to threaten John Johnson, but so far as we know never did actually try to kill him. The fact that Johnson was married to Hole-in-the-Day's cousin didn't seem to be a deterrent.

Following Hole-in-the-Day's aborted attack, Major Walker, the local Indian agent, fled to Fort Ripley. He did not stay there long because he feared its meager defenses would not withstand an attack by Hole-in-the-Day's forces. He headed for Fort Snelling and on his way met the U.S. Commissioner for Indian Affairs, William Dole, in the village of St. Cloud. He told him that Indian forces were about to attack Fort Ripley and that in his opinion the Whites didn't have a chance. Dole then contacted Governor Ramsey and persuaded him to send 300 soldiers to protect the fort.

Meanwhile Walker continued his journey to Fort Snelling along with a handful of "half-breeds" for his protection. His body was later found between Big Lake and Monticello. He had been shot in the head, apparently with his own gun. The protectors were gone; so were all his valuables. It

Oua-wi-sain-shish (Bad Boy). He may have been "Bad Boy" to Hole-in-the-Day but he was a hero to the Whites of central Minnesota.

Courtesy Crow Wing County Historical Society

has never been decided whether his death was suicide or homicide.

There are several versions of what happened next. This is not unusual in trying to recapture history. Even among people who were present, there are normally different perceptions of what took place, and time sometimes changes our memories. In examining several accounts, we have tried to piece together just what happened and in what sequence. Much of what follows is taken from the eyewitness version of George Sweet, a resident at that time of the Sauk Rapids area and a member of the state legislature. Other sources were Nathan Butler's report to the Minnesota State Historical Society and the findings of WPA researchers in the 1930s.

It should be noted that prior to the Pillager uprising the relationship between Hole-in-the-Day and Indian agent Walker had become very hostile. On a trip to Washington, D.C. on another matter the chief had tried, but failed, to get rid of Walker. The feud escalated and Walker secured a contingent of soldiers for the purpose of arresting Hole-in-the-Day. The chief saw them coming and escaped across the river under a hail of fire.

There had also been a history of late payments to the Indians and confusion over where they were to received their payments. Hole-in-the-Day perceived a general depreciation of the quality of life of his people while, in the meantime, the area was changing greatly as the beautiful timber was being logged off and Whites were beginning to settle in the area. The chief was well aware that the Civil War was not going well for the North. He was a very intelligent man and knew that he was in an excellent position to bargain for his people, particularly as the Dakota Sioux went on the rampage in the Mankato-New Ulm area.

U.S. Indian Commissioner William Dole was aware that the situation at Gull Lake was escalating and asked George Sweet to meet with him in the new town of St. Cloud. Butler, a government surveyor had just come from the area and he joined the other two. Agent Walker, as mentioned earlier, was fleeing to what he thought was the only safe place left in Minnesota: Fort Snelling. (He never made it). Walker arrived in St. Cloud as the meeting was taking place. Butler and Walker updated Dole and Sweet on developments at Gull Lake, including the arrival of a small army of Pillagers from Leech Lake with white captives and the burning of the missions.

It was determined that Sweet, who was a good and long time friend of Hole-in-the-Day, should go directly to Gull Lake and try to persuade the chief to back down. To give Sweet greater clout, it was determined that he could say he was Commissioner Dole's personal representative.

Sweet met Chief Bad Boy and Peter Roy*, a government interpreter

*Peter Roy later operated an inn at Old Wadena on the Crow Wing River.

and legislator, on his way north, between Fort Ripley and the village of Crow Wing. They were returning from a meeting with Hole-in-the-Day in which Bad Boy had made it quite clear that he would fight on the side of the Whites if necessary. Both men felt they had failed in trying to persuade Hole-in-the-Day to back down and urged Sweet to turn around. Later reports would indicate that Bad Boy had more impact than he thought and even though there was enmity between the two chiefs, Hole-in-the-Day took Bad Boy's warning seriously in making his final decision.

At Crow Wing, Sweet sought out Clement Beaulieu, the trader, and persuaded him to go along to see Hole-in-the-Day. Beaulieu had done business with the chief and Sweet believed he would be helpful. They hired a driver and team to take them to Hole-in-the-Day's camp, but walked the last half-mile.

Sweet gave the following account of what happened as they advanced past an armed guard.

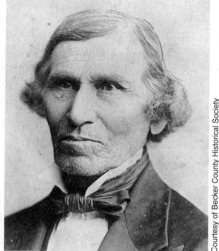

Courtesy of Becker County Historical Society

Clement Hudon Beaulieu (1811-1892), famed trader and one of the founders of Old Crow Wing. He talked sense to Hole-in-the-Day

There followed a terrific war whoop and a whole force of armed Indians seemed to come out of the ground. They numbered about 300 and were armed with rifles, Nor' west guns, war clubs, tomahawks, scalping knives, and a few had scythes to which they had fitted handles like corn cutters. Crowding our way through the excited mass, our party came to Hole-in-the-Day's stronghold, distinguished from the other wigwams by a flagstaff in front flying a small flag, not the stars and stripes, however, but one of their own making. A proud and haughty Hole-in-the-Day emerged. His face, paler than usual, was set, and in his eyes we could discover no sign of welcome, such as I had become accustomed to receive on meeting him.

At my request he ordered his warriors to move back and give us room, whereupon they formed a semi-circle. All were seated. I stated that I had come to see the chief and to learn from his own mouth what his complaints were and whether he wanted war or peace with the Whites.

The chief replied that he did not want war, only his rights; that he could not get his rights by peaceful means; that government agents were actually stealing from his people; that new traders were brought into the country purposefully and in partnership with the agent; that his people were not only forced to trade with these men, but that the Indians' goods were placed in the trader's store to be re-obtained by the Indians at a price these men set. Was this fair?

Sweet replied that justice could not be obtained by force and suggested that an investigative task force be appointed. He assured the chief that as Dole's representative he would make sure the commissioner heard the complaints. He then asked Hole-in-the-Day, as a demonstration of good faith, to release the prisoners. He promised that in return the soldiers would no longer try to capture the chief. He suggested a four-day truce to give him an opportunity to meet with Dole.

The chief agreed.

Sweet and Beaulieu returned to Fort Ripley where the commandant agreed to honor the four-day truce. That same night Sweet went on to Little Falls. On the way he met Captain Beaulieu* and Captain Hall who were on their way to Fort Ripley to take charge there. Sweet briefed them and they also promised to honor the truce. Sweet then reported to Dole, who agreed to meet with Hole-in-the-Day but wanted at least two companies of troops for his protection. Sweet persuaded Governor Ramsey to provide the soldiers from Fort Snelling. It took a few days to make the troops available, so Sweet went back to Hole-in-the-Day to ask for an extension of the truce. Dole wanted the chief to come to the conference on his terms and said that it would be held at Fort Ripley. The chief saw through the strategy and refused. In the end, the confab was held between Gull Lake and the agency. When Dole and the troops arrived they found they were badly out-numbered and surrounded. Sensing the dilemma in which he found himself, Dole opened the ceremony by addressing the Pillagers as "my dear red brethren." It was a wise choice of words and eased the tension.

Dole later described the chief as "insolent"; he was further upset by the fact he had been out-numbered and out-maneuvered. He ordered no further distribution of goods or food to the Ojibwe until approved by the superintendent.

Dole did not know it at the time, but although he had lost the moment, he would be the winner in the long term. That night, after the Whites had left, the Ojibwe from the other parts of northern Minnesota accused Hole-in-the-Day of gaining nothing for all their efforts. The prisoners were gone, the Whites were angry and afraid and the representatives of the American government were upset with the Ojibwe.

We don't know if he was related to Clement Beaulieu.

Hole-in-the-Day was even questioned about his stewardship of past government payments. Later that night (September 12) and the next morning the three other Pillager chiefs and their men crossed the river to the agency where they announced to Agent Morrill that they were leaving Hole-in-the-Day and were going home. They turned in the horses and other loot they had taken from the Whites and in return were given food and supplies from the agency. There were 364 Leech Lake Pillager warriors in all.

At about this time, Father Pierz, who had a church in Old Crow Wing and who was a very good friend of Hole-in-the-Day, decided to do what he could to persuade the Chief to cooperate with Agent Dole. He traveled all alone to Hole-in-the-Day's headquarters. As he drew near, he was met by Pillager warriors who were guarding the trail. They told the priest that he could go no further. They pointed to a line drawn in the sand and announced that anyone who stepped across it would be killed. Pierz replied, "Well, then, carry me across." The Indians complied!

Hole-in-the-Day had allowed Father Pierz to baptize his children and had even had discussions with the priest about his own possible conversion. The two men were, in fact, good friends. Father Pierz later would say that the greeting he received from the chief was anything but friendly. But as they talked and as the priest pointed out the folly of fighting the Whites, assuring the chief that the army would come and kill many of his tribe, the chief softened and in the end extended his hand to Father Pierz and said, "We will make peace."

No one individual can take full credit for deterring Hole-in-the-Day from his mission. All of the above can take some credit, including the Leech Lake Pillagers who deserted him.

Just before the Leech Lake Ojibwe headed home, the Minnesota State Legislature went into special session because of the Sioux conflict. There was also grave concern about what Hole-in-the-Day might do. A special commission was established to meet with the Ojibwe. Only the Ojibwe under Hole-in-the-Day's command attended the subsequent conference at Old Crow Wing; by then the Leech Lake band had arrived home.

Only the United States Government has the power to execute treaties, but the document that came out of the conference took that form. It was signed by the members of the commission and the Ojibwe leadership. The treaty pretty much provided for peace and the status quo, but Dole and local Indian agent, Morrill, were very upset, for two reasons: (1) they felt the state was usurping their powers as agents of the federal government and (2) they believed the Indians should have been punished for their threatened insurrection.

Actually, in the end, the "treaty" wasn't that significant. In six short years the Gull Lake-Crow Wing-Mississippi band of Pillagers would be moved to the White Earth reservation.

We will never know just how close this area may have come to all out war. Surely the combined forces of the Ojibwe far outnumbered the Whites and soldiers. Yet, in reading Sweet's description of Hole-in-the-Day's warriors some were described as brandishing very primitive weapons. No doubt the situation was delicate enough that even the accidental firing of a gun at any of the conferences could have resulted in much bloodshed. So was Hole-in-the-Day bluffing and organizing this great show of strength to improve his chances of negotiating better things for his people? Or was he ready to go to war if that was what it took? We'll never know, but the wily chief had a long history of "brinksmanship" – threatening and blustering but rarely resorting to violence when Whites were involved. There was also the long history of the chief developing true friendships with individual Whites and being very helpful to others on many occasions. We'll just never know.

After the threatened 1862 uprising, things were never the same in our central lakes area. Hole-in-the-Day remained principal chief but he had lost some of his clout. For example, a handful of hostile Whites felt brave enough to burn down his beautiful Crow Wing home. Meanwhile, there was a move, nationally, to place all Indians on reservations.

In 1863, Hole-in-the-Day signed a treaty ceding all his domain to the United States in exchange for a reservation in the Leech Lake – Cass Lake region. The Ojibwe of our area then had second thoughts and refused to move. Then in 1864 the Leech-Cass reservation was created but the Pillagers of our area, including Mille Lacs Lake, were allowed to stay where they were. As part of this treaty, Hole-in-the-Day was given $5,000 to restore his home. Then in 1867, a new treaty provided for the creation of a reservation at White Earth (near Mahnomen) and the Pillagers of the area we have been studying were ordered to move there. The Mille Lacs Ojibwe complained, reminding the representative of the U.S. Government that this was not the way to treat the friends of the Whites who had stood up to Hole-in-the-Day back in 1862. The government agreed, but the rest of the Ojibwe in the area had to move.

THE EXODUS

Even though Hole-in-the-Day had signed the treaty he had a change of heart and ordered his people not to go. He was also upset that mixed-bloods would be able to move to the reservation. The fact that the vast majority of his people did go showed that the chief had lost still more of his clout. John Johnson (Enmegahbowh) in another letter to Judge Nathan Richardson of Little Falls describes the exodus and Hole-in-the-Day's opposition:

The chiefs and the old men and women often come and ask if I knew anything about their removal. I said out openly, "Yes, I think that very thing must come to affect us, because the government has and is still removing the different Indian tribes all over the United States, for some cause, a good cause. It is always a good cause, because the government makes it to become such. Here it is. Just see it. Bye-and-bye, I say, you all shall be removed. Now if you ask me why, if you have done anything to justify your removal, look back a year ago. See what you have done, and the warriors who came and were ready to make a general warfare against your friends the whites. My friends, had I not been a living man, mark you, when you started to go on with the warfare, had I not interfered, today all you people would not have walked on your beautiful ground nor paddled your canoes on these beautiful lakes and rivers. You would have been destroyed and swept away from the face of the earth. And for saving you and interfering, you wanted to kill me, and you would have done it had I not escaped from my home you would have killed me. In doing the above I showed my love toward you. You are all here, smoking your pipe of peace. You ought to thank me for it. And for this very foolish act of yours the government will say to you all you must remove.

Sure enough, on the next year following the most dreadful word reached the ears of my people. "You must be removed toward the setting sun, near to the country of your great heredity enemies." To describe the feelings and sayings of my people would fill many sheets of paper. I will pass them over and will give you a few items that actually occurred. Hole-in-the-Day took up against the cause, and advised his people not to move. He was very bitter against it, and even threatened death to the first man who would not give heed to his words. He must surely die. The day was named on which they must be ready to move. Hole-in-the-Day got ready, and sent four of his best warriors to the road to watch and intercept the first man who may pass and to halt him. The warriors started to do as they were commanded. Chief Turtle or Na-bun-a-skong were to lead the caravan. He was considered one of the bravest and most daring warriors. He walked ahead of the moving caravan, feathers waving on his head, and singing the war song. Here were Hole-in-the-Day's braves watching the moving caravan come on, two of the braves standing on each side of the road. Sure enough, here came the moving caravan, and Chief Na-bun-a-skong saw them watching. When he saw them standing on both sides of the road, he made a loud war whoop, as much as to say, "I, too, am a brave and warrior!" Everybody thought it would cause much trouble and bloodshed; and as the chief was nearing them, and passing, he thought he would be shot down every moment. But he passed through without any effort on their part to stop him. After the first move took place, Hole-in-the-Day saw that his work was not heeded nor noticed. He gave up the cause; and yet there was one more item that he will never overlook, and that he must attend to himself, personally, and without fail, and that is to make his final settlement with Enmegahbowh, the treacherous man.

Thus the removal took place without any trouble. My poor people have gone away broken hearted. I pitied the poor women most, and felt much sympathy for them. I never can forget what Na-bun-a-skong did before his final step took place for the unknown country. Looking at the deep pine forest, with his hands stretched forth, and with a deep voice he said, "O you majestic pine forest, how often have I sought shelter and protection under thy great wing! Thy songs have often cheered me and thy waving heads have halted me to listen to their melodious songs. Oh, you majestic pine forest! Continue to sing thy beautiful songs, to awaken and to cheer my dear children that I have left behind me in their graves!" Turning toward the Mississippi and pointing to it he said, "Oh ye, the father of rivers, for ages past thy beautiful current has often cheered me while gliding over thy currents with my canoe! I am leaving thee! I shall never again grace thy flowing waters. I leave thee, not by my wish, but I am compelled." And again pointing towards the mountain, he said, with a loud voice, "Oh, you beautiful mount! How often have I hidden under thy walls when in danger!" So saying he returned, much cast down and with spirits of melancholy. He was the most earnest advocate that I should move with them. But, at the same time, he knew well that it was not safe for me to move with them when the loaded gun was pointed at me. Again and again I said that the Great Spirit would open the door for me to enter into their country.

THE MURDER OF CHIEF HOLE-IN-THE-DAY THE YOUNGER

Chief Hole-in-the-Day was assassinated on July 9, 1868* on a trail along Gull River. Normally he traveled with an interpreter who also served as bodyguard. On this occasion, his traveling companion was an interpreter named "Ojibwa" but he was unarmed, as was the chief. He was ambushed and shot by a party of eleven* young Pillagers from Leech Lake. Supposedly his last words were, "You have me at a disadvantage; I am unarmed."

The motive is unclear. Six years earlier, the Leech Lake Pillagers had deserted Hole-in-the-Day and went home in a huff during the threatened uprising in 1862, but it is difficult to imagine that those hard feel-

Some sources list other dates in July and August
Some sources list as few as two assassins; other sources say nine.

ings had continued for that many years or that they were serious enough to warrant his murder. The chief did have his share of enemies, both White and Indian, and he had threatened to kill others. Some thought it was murder for hire. It was rumored that Clement Beaulieu, Sr., George Fairbanks, Bill McArthur and John Morrison (all of Crow Wing) paid to have him killed. Others thought the Leech Lake braves were hired by Crow Wing "half-breeds" who were angry with Hole-in-the-Day because he opposed their move to the White Earth Reservation.

The actual murderers were known, but never punished.

The chief's traveling companion was not harmed. The killers took him with them to the chief's home. They threatened the wives but Ojibwa talked the Pillagers out of doing them harm. They returned to Leech Lake.

At the time of his death, Hole-in-the-Day had five wives. Three were Ojibwe, one was Sioux, and the other, Helen Kater, was White. He had met the latter in 1867 when he was in Washington, D.C. negotiating a treaty. She was working at the hotel where he stayed. He married her and brought her back to Minnesota. It is unfortunate that there are no records of what her impressions were of this foreign setting! After Hole-in-the-Day's death, she moved to Minneapolis and found work. She took her infant son (by Hole-in-the-Day) with her. The child was adopted by a family named "Woodbury" and took that name; his first name was John.

Hole-in-the-Day III. His given Ojibwe name was Mino-Geshig ("Five Day"); his English name was Ignatius.

Courtesy Crow Wing County Historical Society

Hole-in-the-Day III (Ignatius), as the oldest brother, inherited his father's lands, including the northeast shore of Gull Lake. He graduated from St. John's University in 1874 and was fluent in four languages. For a time he was leader of the Ojibwe on the White Earth Reservation. He joined the Hale and Bigelow Medicine Show and was murdered while in Chicago, November 15, 1888. His body was found in the north branch of the Chicago River. Following his death, his younger brother, John (Hole-in-the-Day IV) Woodbury, whose mother was white, moved with his family to White Earth where he assumed the rank of chief.

Hole-in-the-Day's Sioux wife was so upset with her husband when he brought home a white wife that she moved out, along with her son. She had been the Chief's favorite. Legend has it that she finally committed suicide by jumping off Dutchman's Bluff on Gull Lake.

Hole-in-the-Day had seven children. In addition to the three sons we have mentioned (Ignatius, John and the son of the Sioux wife) there were four daughters. Isabelle, who married William Warren, Louise, who married a man named Roberts, Adeline, who married John Fairbanks and Oh-bezzum who married Peter Jordan. None of Hole-in-the-Day's children lived beyond middle age.

Hole-in-the-Day was only forty years old when he was murdered. He was buried in the Catholic cemetery in Crow Wing with a cross as his headstone. This raises an interesting question: was the chief Catholic? After all, Father Pierz had baptized at least two of his daughters: their baptismal names were Mary Antoinette and Maria Francois (at his church in Belle Prairie). We do know that the chief and father Pierz were good friends and that they had several conversations about spiritual things. One story is that the priest authorized his burial in the church cemetery because of those conversations. An exhaustive search of the records of the St. Cloud Diocese, however, revealed no record of his baptism. One theory is that he was buried just over the cemetery boundary.

Hole-in-the-Day was a remarkable man. He packed a very full life into his 40 years. He surely was a great leader of his people and he tried to improve their living conditions. While honoring his own culture, he coveted for his people the quality of living enjoyed by the Whites. In his later years he lived as a well-to-do man of any race. The picture of him on the cover of this book is so appropriate. It shows Hole-in-the-Day dressed in both White and Indian attire. While loyal to Ojibwe ways, he lived in Whiteman's style houses and was proud of his success as a farmer on the Gull River.

Although he could not read or write, he had newspapers read to him regularly. He was a highly intelligent, charismatic, powerful leader.

He had traveled several times to Washington, D.C. and was known nationally. His death was reported in newspapers across the country.

THE END OF THE 100 YEARS DAKOTA-OJIBWE WAR

The 100 Years War came to an end because the white military forces drove the Sioux out of the state during the 1862 uprising. The next year (1863) the military marched into the Dakotas and most of the Sioux fled farther west or north into Canada.

Warren's first wife, Mathilda, was the daughter of Aitkin, the white trader. He married her when he was eighteen. She re-married after his death. It is not certain that Hole-in-the-Day's daughter, Isabelle, was also married to William Warren, the author and legislator; it may have been a different William Warren. We will continue to research this question.

With the exception of the peaceful Mdewakanton Sioux in southeastern Minnesota, the Ojibwe were the only Native American people left in the state; there was no one to fight. Relatively small numbers of Sioux eventually returned to Minnesota. At this writing the Sioux operate very profitable casinos in Shakopee, Red Wing and Morton.

We cannot even venture a guess as to how many Dakotas and Ojibwe lost their lives during the century-long conflict. Surely there were thousands—men, women, and even children. It was the practice of both the Dakotas and the Ojibwe to kill everyone, hoping to totally eliminate their enemies. We can only imagine the pain and suffering endured by families as individuals were killed – not to mention those wounded and maimed. Sometimes whole villages were obliterated.

Tragically, as with most wars, it was all for naught; nothing really changed. From the ousting of the Dakotas from the woodlands in 1766 to the end of the conflict in 1862, the Dakotas did not take back one inch of the Minnesota woodlands, nor were the Ojibwe able to expand their territory into the prairies. In more than 100 years of fighting, nothing was gained; everyone lost.

The remaining chapters will deal with "the times" of our three leaders. In these chapters we will also have the opportunity to learn more about the three charismatic chiefs: Curly Head and the two Hole-in-the-Days.

CHAPTER V

The Winnebago (Ho-chunk) Reservation

For seven years, as the Dakota Sioux – Ojibwe war was winding down, an area of 900,000 acres south of the Crow Wing and Long Prairie Rivers was home to the Winnebago Sioux Indians. Hole-in-the-Day II made it possible.

When the first European settlers arrived in the Midwest in the 1800s they found the Winnebago's in what is now southern Wisconsin and northern Illinois. It is estimated that at that time they numbered about 5,000. We do not know a great deal about their earlier history but it seems as though they were always fighting with some other tribe – even other Sioux tribes. The Winnebago's occasionally had allies but they usually ended up at odds with them too. This was especially true of their relationship with their cousins, the Fox. One year they would be allies; the next year they would be fighting each other. There are even accounts of the Winnebago's fighting among themselves, one village against another.

As white farmers sought homesteads in what is now Wisconsin and Illinois, they coveted the land occupied by the Winnebago's. In an 1837 treaty, the tribe agreed to move farther west and by 1842 occupied the southeast tip of what is now Minnesota. They also settled along the Mississippi River in what is now Iowa – but not for long. As "would be" farmers discovered the rich, black soil in the new Winnebago homeland, pressure was applied on the U.S. Government to move the Indians once again.

The Winnebago's were told they could have a new land of their choosing in what is now Minnesota north of the St. Peter (Minnesota) River and west of the Mississippi. Because of the long war between the Dakotas and the Ojibwe this area was sparsely settled and the government saw an opportunity to create a buffer between the Dakotas and the Ojibwe.

The land purchase agreement was spelled out in the Treaty of 1847; it was negotiated and signed at Fond du Lac. Chief Hole-in-the-Day II (the younger) represented the Ojibwe. He met with the U.S. land commissioners first by himself and worked out the details. He then left and returned with a number of Ojibwe chiefs. With the entourage standing behind him, he made this little speech:

> *Dear Fathers, the country our Great Father wants to purchase belongs to me. If I say sell, our Great Father will have it. If I say not sell, he will go without it. These Indians you see behind me have nothing to say about it. I approve the treaty and will sign it and consent to the sale.*

Hole-in-the-Day signed it with an "X" and his name was written both in English and Ojibwe: POO-OO-NE-SHIK.

Hole-in-the-Day had made it very clear to the other chiefs and to the commissioners just who was in charge! This classic example of his big ego helps us understand some of his behavior.

It is significant that the federal government did recognize him as the principal chief of so large an area and that they realized the Ojibwe were winning the war and could lay claim to all of it.

Remember, he was only nineteen or twenty years old!

The Winnebago's were told they could select their own land or choose a representative to select it for them. In addition to having title to the new land, they were to be given $190,000 in cash to help them move and get settled. All of this was stipulated in the Treaty of 1847.

The Winnebago's ended up selecting Henry Rice to choose the location of their new homeland. This is just one of many examples of the high esteem in which this man was held. Not only did the Indians trust him, but the legislature chose Henry Rice as Minnesota's first United States Senator. He is honored to this day with a full-length statue in the United States Capitol. *

William Folwell, in his "History of Minnesota" reported that Rice was given $70 for each Winnebago he delivered to the new reservation. Folwell also reported that he would give Indians a small sum of money to disappear for a while; he supposedly received another $70 when he brought them back. Other sources reported a similar scheme but stated a smaller fee: $30. If true, these stories cast a shadow on his reputation and the integrity he demonstrated as a U.S. Senator.

Rice mapped out 898,000 acres of land, "beginning at the junction of the Crow Wing and Mississippi Rivers; thence up the Crow Wing to the Long Prairie River; thence up that river to the boundary line between the Sioux and the Chippewa's; then southerly along said boundary to a

*Each state is entitled to two statues in the Capitol building. Minnesota's other statue is Maria Sanford, the first female professor at the University of Minnesota. Each Vice President is entitled to a bust; Minnesota has Hubert Humphrey and Walter Mondale. Chief Flat Mouth of Leech Lake also has a bust in the capital (see page 33).

lake (Carlos) at the head of the Long Prairie River; thence in a direct line to the Watab River; thence down the Watab River to the Mississippi River; thence up the Mississippi to the beginning" (Old Crow Wing). Rice was also the one who then negotiated the purchase of this land from the Ojibwe – with none other than Chief Hole-in-the-Day II.

The Winnebago's did not use all of the $190,000 they were allocated for moving expenses and for the construction of homes and other necessary buildings. Eighty-five thousand dollars remained and this was placed in trust at 5% interest.

There was talk of the Menomonee Indians of Wisconsin moving into the area north of Long Prairie and later of replacing the Winnebago's when they left, but neither happened, even though a treaty was negotiated.

In 1848, the Winnebago's began their journey north to their promised land. The move was not without difficulties. Many had second thoughts about the 1847 treaty. There were deserters all along the way. The military escort proved too small to keep them in line. Less than half the tribe arrived in the new homeland. Large numbers decided to go to Wisconsin, where they were welcomed by Chief Wabasha. Others scattered themselves from Iowa to Nebraska. Rice had to call on the military stationed at Fort Snelling to move the remainder north. The Bureau of Indian Affairs helped by saying there would be no payment of annuities except at the new agency at what is now the city of Long Prairie.

When the caravan arrived at Swan River, Chief Hole-in-the-Day II met them there. He said that he had changed his mind about giving up the land and tried to turn them back. It was Henry Rice who finally talked the chief into backing down. By early August, the move was finally completed. As we have already said, the agency buildings were constructed where the City of Long Prairie now stands, but the Winnebago's scattered themselves all over the 900,000 acres with concentrations in the north at Long Prairie and in the south along the Watab River.

Some of the Winnebago's made a sincere and somewhat successful effort at farming. Although the farms were more like large gardens, it was recorded that there were 250 acres under cultivation in 1849, 455 acres in 1850, 500 acres in 1851 and 500 acres in 1852. The next year (1853) some of the Indians started moving out of the area so the acreage was considerably less. The major crops were wheat, oats, corn, potatoes and turnips. A gristmill was constructed. The Winnebago's proved they could farm but complained about the light, sandy soil. They also were unhappy because of all the trees; they preferred, and were used to, open prairies.

Buildings sprang up that first year, including agency offices, a school, boarding house, a Catholic church, stables, three trading posts, 35 Indian houses, a house for the physician and a house for the official interpreter.

Many Whites were attracted to the reservation. Some worked for the government; others were missionaries, traders, merchants etc. By 1849, there were two newspapers published on the reservation: "the Pioneer" and "the Watab Review". They were two of the first, if not the first, newspapers in the Minnesota Territory! By 1850, the Long Prairie part of the reservation had about 250 buildings. It was estimated that the total population that year (all races) was nearly 3,000. That same year, St. Paul had a population of less than 800 and Minneapolis did not yet exist. Clearly, it was the major population center of the state. It is little wonder that the second road (not just an improved trail) constructed in Minnesota was from Swan River (where it enters the Mississippi) to Long Prairie. It was paid for with federal dollars. Later, it was extended west to Fort Ridgely. The very first road built in the state was from Fort Snelling to Fort Ripley. It was later extended to Old Crow Wing. A road from St. Paul to Lake Superior was supposed to have been first, but was delayed because of a controversy over where is should hit the lake. It did become the third road built, however.

Indian agents were political appointees. The first agent was a Democrat, Jonathan Fletcher; he was replaced by Fridley, a Whig, but returned two years later when the Democrats regained power.

In addition to the three trading posts in Long Prairie, there were two on the Watab River. This was quite a concentration of trading posts, but as we have said several times, this area was known for its excellent hunting and trapping. The records of one of the posts for the 1852 season have been preserved: they recorded 207 raccoon, 1608 muskrat, 15 otter, 89 mink, 10 fisher, 4 martin, 6 red fox, 1 gray fox, 10 wolves and 10 bear. The total amount paid out in cash and supplies was $396.45. The absence of any beaver in the list is a puzzle. It may be that other traders were paying more for them. Since it was beaver that drew traders to the area originally it is not likely they were all trapped out, although Cadotte and his men did trap or purchase more than 12,000 beaver pelts in a single season!

On at least one occasion, hostilities broke out between the Winnebago's and the Pillagers. Two of Hole-in-the-Day's men were killed by a small band of intoxicated Winnebago's. Father De Vivaldi, who was stationed at the mission on the reservation, feared an escalation of the violence and sent word to Father Pierz at Crow Wing, asking for his help. He knew of his many contacts with the Ojibwe and his friendship with Hole-in-the-Day II. Pierz hastened to the reservation where he intercepted a Pillager sub-chief, Attawan, and some of his warriors bent on revenge. The priest was able to persuade the members of both tribes of the folly of further bloodshed. When the Pillagers agreed to go home in peace, Father De Vivaldi gave them some domestic meat and the Winnebago's provided a gift of tobacco.

The extensive missionary efforts across the Winnebago reservation were actually the first in what is now the State of Minnesota. The Reverend David Lowry, an Episcopalian, was the first to arrive. He also filled in as Superintendent of schools for a time; so much for separation of church and state!

Bishop Cretin, stationed in St. Paul, established a Catholic church at present day Long Prairie; the first priest was Father DeVivaldi and the first nun Sister Scholastica. Later, Sisters O'Brien and Appolonia were stationed at the mission. In the latter's report to Bishop Cretin, she spoke of the difficult four day journey from St. Paul. She also reported sleeping on hay in the attic of their small, log home and how frightened they were at first by all the singing and dancing of the Winnebago's most nights. In the census of 1849, only 39 of the entire population of 2,551 Indians were identified as "professing Christians", but the census reported that 233 attended Sunday school. As with later reservations, "conversions" came slowly indeed; however, once Native Americans were ordained, it made quite a difference.

Because of all the stores and trading posts located at what is now Long Prairie, the Mille Lacs Lake Ojibwe, including Chief Bad Boy, were frequent visitors. In fact, during the uprisings of 1862, Bad Boy adopted the family of A.D. Brower and stationed some of his men at their homestead to protect them against the Sioux. Occasionally Dakota war parties did get as close as present day Sauk Center.

The Winnebago's never were really happy with the location of their reservation and in 1853 a new treaty was negotiated which would have moved the tribe to the Crow Wing, but in the end neither the United States Senate nor the Winnebago's ratified it. *

In 1855, however, the Winnebago's were moved to the Blue Earth Reservation near Mankato. There were three major reasons for the move: (1) the Winnebago's never were happy in their northern home, (2) there were occasional skirmishes with the neighboring Ojibwe under the leadership of Hole-in-the-Day II and (3) white settlers were interested in farming the area.

After the Winnebago's moved south, a few Whites remained, but by 1860, nearly all had moved away. Soldiers were stationed in the area for a time to protect the settlers should Hole-in-the-Day try to reclaim the area, but they were not needed as nearly all Whites left the area. Almost all of the buildings disappeared within two years after the closing of the

*Edward J. Pluth of the St. Cloud State University faculty has written an excellent article about the Watab Treaty in the spring 2000 edition of "Minnesota History." Pluth's master's degree thesis is a detailed history of the Winnebago Reservation.

reservation. Some were burned, others were dismantled by the Whites who stayed in the area and the lumber was used to build houses and barns. The major immigration of European settlers did not begin until 1866.

After the Dakota Sioux uprising in 1862, the Winnebago's were once again forced to move; this time they were scattered across southern Wisconsin, Nebraska and, for a time, South Dakota. Census records indicate that about 500 Winnebago's now live in Minnesota.

At first, the new town of Long Prairie was known as "Liberty Pole." On July 4, 1860, the twenty some Whites living in the area gathered at a spot where the courthouse now stands to celebrate the birth of our nation. They erected a flagpole in honor of the occasion and called their simple monument "Liberty Pole." As the town began to develop and grow they called the new community by that name.

CHAPTER VI

Fort Ripley

If the Winnebago's had not moved to Long Prairie and if there hadn't been deep concern about the need to keep Hole-in-the-Day's Ojibwe and the Winnebago's at peace with each other and if there had not been a need to protect Whites as they moved into the area, there would never have been a Fort Ripley. The 100 Years War between the Dakota and the Ojibwe had begun to wind down but the Winnebago's were a Sioux tribe and since Hole-in-the-Day had expressed second thoughts about selling his land for a Winnebago reservation, there was legitimate concern that fighting could break out. Chief Hole-in-the-Day and Chief Bad Boy, of Mille Lacs Lake, were continually threatening each other. Then, with white settlers beginning to come into the area in significant numbers, it was determined by the federal government that a fort had to be built at a location near the Winnebago reservation but also close to Old Crow Wing.

In 1848, the Secretary of War commissioned Brig. General G.M. Brooke to choose the location. The site he chose was seven miles below the mouth of the Crow Wing on the Mississippi River. The Adjutant General authorized Brooke to select two parcels of land; one on the west bank for the location of the fort, and a larger parcel across the river to be used for agricultural purposes and harvesting firewood. President Zachary Taylor made it official in 1849, setting aside a military reservation consisting of one square mile (about 1,000 acres) on the west bank and one area four miles deep by ten miles along the east bank (later surveyed as 57,618.5 acres) starting across from the mouth of the Crow Wing River and running south along the Mississippi.

A company of soldiers and fifteen laborers under the supervision of a Captain Dana arrived in the fall of 1848. They came by steamboat from St. Louis as far as Fort Snelling, bringing with them horses, cattle, tools and building supplies. Here, they transferred everything (except the livestock) to wagons and proceeded up the east side of the river to the Crow Wing trading post across the Mississippi from the mouth of the

Crow Wing River. They followed the cart trails but it was not much of a road for horse-drawn wagons and the journey took nine days. More soldiers arrived a little later, supposedly to help protect the workers from possible hostile Indians. Apparently it was decided that the Indians were not a threat, because just before freeze-up the soldiers all went back downriver to the comforts of Fort Snelling.

During the winter, the laborers cut construction logs. One of the workers, Charles T. Stearn, reported that a horse-powered sawmill with a circular saw was used to make some of the logs into lumber.

On April 13, 1849, the military returned and actual construction commenced. With the fort and its soldiers for protection, a few Whites came up river and began settling around the Crow Wing trading post.

At first, the fort was called Fort Gaines, but when it was learned that another fort already had that name, it was renamed Fort Ripley. *

In 1851, Reverend Solon W. Meanney arrived. He served for several years as chaplain and also taught school (the pupils were children of settlers and soldiers). His diaries provide an excellent source of information about life at the fort.

In 1851, Fort Ripley rated its own surgeon in residence, Dr. Alexander B. Hansen.

The following is a description of the fort in 1856 as taken from the doctor's diary:

On the west side of the river is Fort Ripley, with quarters, barracks, etc. all built of wood, enclosed on three sides by the buildings, and on the fourth by the river, a quadrangle piece of ground of about three acres, beautifully ornamented. The houses of the officers, built facing each other, forming two right angles from the river, are cottage style with a wide piazza, and are altogether very comfortable and convenient. All the buildings are kept handsomely painted, the ground neat and clean, which makes the fort present from the river, a very pleasant and comfortable appearance. Nor is the appearance deceitful to a visitor at the fort or at the quarters of the officers.

Rev. Meanney's diary indicates that although the fort was built to keep the Indians at peace, there were actually more arrests of Whites— including a young man who took the life of a black man at Swan River in 1852 and the arrests of four men who set Beaulieu's trading post at Crow Wing on fire in 1858.

Father Ezekiel Gear, who replaced Rev. Meanney in 1860, reported that there were very few settlers in the area and that they "survived mostly by selling whiskey to the Indians".

Famous missionaries and preachers who visited the fort included Father De Vivaldi (Catholic), Edward Neill (Presbyterian), and two Episcopalians: James Breck and E. Steele Peake.

Edmund P. Gaines was a Brigadier General, then stationed at New Orleans. General James W. Ripley had distinguished himself in the War of 1812 and later served in congress.

With the construction of Fort Ridgely on the upper Minnesota River and with the Winnebago's being moved to Blue Earth in 1855, there was less need for Fort Ripley and it was abandoned in July of 1857. However, no sooner had the military left than some of Hole-in-the-Day's men went on a rampage. As mentioned earlier, they killed a settler (a trader of sorts) and according to one report, burned out several others. Chief Bad Boy, who was then still living on Gull Lake, captured the culprits and took them to Fort Ripley with the intention of turning them over to the military. To his surprise, he found the soldiers had moved to Fort Snelling, so he then turned them over to the sheriff of the tiny settlement at Little Falls. The sheriff put them in chains and headed for Fort Snelling. An armed band of Whites overtook the sheriff and relieved him of his prisoners. They returned with them as far as Swan River where they hanged them and buried them still chained together. As reported earlier, Hole-in-the-Day (the Younger) never forgave Bad Boy for his role in capturing his warriors and threatened to kill him. It was also at this time that the federal government once again recognized Hole-in-the-Day as Principal Chief of the Gull Lake—Crow Wing—and Mississippi Ojibwe. That was "the last straw" for Chief Bad Boy and he moved his village to Mille Lacs Lake. As a result of all this, the soldiers were brought back to Fort Ripley.

It was certainly fortunate that the fort was in operation during the threatened Pillager uprising in 1862. As we have already discussed, a Sioux uprising took place at that same time along the Minnesota River. That conflict ended with all, or nearly all of the Dakota Sioux being driven from the state. Just before the outbreak of hostilities in the southern part of the state, a contingent of military from Fort Ripley had ridden to Fort Ridgely because of rumors of troubles. It was decided they were not needed so they returned to Fort Ripley. They were on their way back as fighting broke out.

As reported in previous chapters, with the burning of the Episcopal mission on Gull Lake and the Lutheran mission on Lower Mission Lake, the Whites of the area fled to Fort Ripley. They must have been very happy the soldiers had returned to the fort. As we can see from pictures of the fort, it would not have been easily defended. If Hole-in-the-Day and his allies had chosen to attack it is difficult to say who would have won. Those at the fort probably had better weapons and more ammunition, but the Pillagers would have had them badly out-numbered. Of course, with Chief Bad Boy of Mille Lacs Lake and his braves marching to the fort and offering to fight on the side of the Whites, that may very well have more than evened the odds. At any rate, with the signing of the peace agreement everyone must have breathed easier!

With peace restored both in the nation and in the Minnesota heart-

Artist's rendition of Fort Ripley

Courtesy Minnesota Historical Society

land, there was little need for Fort Ripley; however, troops did remain until 1878. On January 14th of that year, there was a major fire at the fort and the troops all left in July. Even the 52 bodies in the cemetery were removed and re-buried in the federal cemetery in Rock Island, Illinois. A land sale followed, with much of the land going for as little as 10 cents an acre. Good lumber was scarce on the frontier and those buildings which had not burned were salvaged by area settlers.

Camp Ripley was established in the area west of the old fort in 1929; it opened in 1936. It is a permanent installation of the National Guard and upwards of 5,000 men and women receive their training there each year from states as far away as New England and the Deep South. There is also an exchange program with Norway. The camp has a capacity to train over 12,000 troops at one time.

CHAPTER VII
Missionary Efforts

Explorers came here for fame and adventure, traders came for profit but missionaries were only interested in bringing the Good News of the Gospel to the American Indians. The handful of God's servants who unselfishly and courageously worked among the Indians and White settlers in the 17th, 18th and 19th centuries have never received the full credit they deserve for the role they played in the development of our state and nation. Their letters and diaries reveal the hardships and anxieties they suffered. They realized when they came that they very well could be called on to even give their lives, and Father Alneau did in the Lake of the Woods massacre.

In Chapter V, where we talked about the Winnebago Reservation, we described briefly the efforts of Catholics and Episcopalians to establish churches at the north end of the reservation (Long Prairie). We don't know a great deal about the Episcopalian effort, other than that it was headed by Rev. David Lowry and that services were held in the school house and that he also served as superintendent of schools for a time. On the other hand, we know a great deal about the Catholic missionary efforts. We know there was a Catholic church, convent and cemetery. Letters from the nuns to Bishop Cretin survive and some of the contents were given in Chapter Five.

In Minnesota, the Catholics and Episcopalians were usually first to establish Indian missions. The Long Prairie churches were the very first Indian missions in what is now Minnesota for both groups. There was a Lutheran church established a little later on Lower Mission Lake north of Brainerd. You will recall that Chief Hole-in-the-Day's warriors burned it the same time as they destroyed the St. Columba Mission on Gull Lake. The pastor, Rev. Ron Ottomar Cloetter, then established a mission at the village of Crow Wing.

It is interesting that the Catholic sisters came from the Motherhouse of the Sisters of St. Joseph of Carondelet in St. Louis, Missouri, a very long way from Long Prairie, Minnesota.

We gain considerable insight into the trials and tribulations of these early missionaries in the scholarly research and writings of Sister Grace McDonald, O.S.B. of the St. Benedicts Convent in St. Joseph, Minnesota, in which she describes the efforts to establish the Long Prairie Mission.

Before the founding of the mission in St. Paul, the Winnebago Indians had been removed to a place called Long Prairie where the government had located an agency. Many of the Indians were Catholics; and good Bishop Cretin, whose zeal was ever on the alert for the salvation of souls, had secured control of a school established by the government and had sent a priest to take charge of it. The Bishop soon saw that the Indian children should receive more regular instruction than a missionary priest, with his numerous other duties could give them. He thought the Sisters might prove useful auxiliaries. It was then mid-winter, and no Sisters could come from St. Louis until navigation opened in the spring. In this dilemma he conferred with Mother St. John as to the advisability of sending Sisters to teach the Indian girls. They decided on sending one of the four Sisters then at St. Paul to assist in preparing the children for first Holy Communion. Accordingly, Sister Scholastica was chosen and early in January 1852, she left St. Paul for Long Prairie. She was accompanied on her route by Father De Vivaldi, the priest in charge of the Indians. During the time Sister was at the agency, she boarded with the family of Mr. Legeau, whose daughter was the Sister's companion to and from the school, and her assistant in it. After the children had received their first Holy Communion in March, the Sister returned to St. Paul to await the arrival of a companion for her mission.

In June 1852, Rev. Mother Celestine made her first visit to St. Paul, her dear Indian Mission, as she loved to call it. She came from Philadelphia where she had been visiting the Sisters who not long before had gone there from Carondelet. Her companion was Sister Appolonia, who, after remaining in St. Paul a few days to rest, went with Sister Scholastica to Long Prairie. The mission was now, July 1852, considered permanently established and another Sister was to be sent there as soon as possible.

When Mother Celestine returned to St. Louis, Sister Frances Joseph went with her to the Mother House.

In August 1852, two other missionaries arrived. Sister M. Xavier McCusick, who replaced Sister Frances Joseph in the school at St. Paul, and Sister Cesarine O-Brien, who proceeded at once to Long Prairie.

After having spent only six weeks on the Indian mission, Sister Appolonia was recalled to St. Paul. It is to her that I am indebted for the following description of their house or lodge. It had been previously used as a storehouse for the provisions kept on the reservation for the Indians: "It was built of logs and was one story high, the dimensions were about 18 by 20 feet; it contained but one apartment, and that we used for parlor, refectory, community room, and kitchen. Our sleeping room was a very small and low attic. Our mattress was nice clean hay and our bedstead, the floor; over the hay we spread our blankets and comfortables, in truly primitive style." Oh, that was in truth an Indian mission! The weird, wild music of the Indian dance was the last sound the Sisters heard at night; the noisy, savage shriek of the children at play, was the usual after piece to their morning's meditation.

The Indians lived in tents or wigwams. Their children attended school as day pupils. The Sisters taught girls and boys all they were capable of learning—reading, writing, etc. The girls were taught knitting and sewing. All possible efforts were made to civilize them as well as to Christianize them. A man was engaged to teach the boys farming. He had all kinds of agricultural implements and a number of fine horses under his charge; these the Indian boys were taught to use and to care for. The Sisters each received forty dollars per month, the man fifty, and the superintendent sixty. The Sisters attended to the distribution of the provisions which were kept in large storehouses, and given to the Indians on the plan of army rations—each family receiving so much, according to the number of people it contained.

The supplies needed for the use of the mission had to be transported by teams from St. Paul. Teams were the only means of communication between the two places and they made regular trips.

Sisters Scholastica and Cesarine were the only Sisters at Long Prairie during the winter of 1852-1853. They have left us no account of their loneliness, but lonely they must have been, unless their numerous occupations and the novelty of their surroundings prevented them from indulging in lonely reveries. They were daily expecting the arrival of another Sister for their community. Father De Vivaldi was extremely kind to them. They knew that they were working for a good Master, one, who had Himself suffered poverty, hardship and loneliness. They offered all to Him and were content.

Early in the spring of 1853, Sisters Victorine and Simeon came to Minnesota. Sister Victorine, who was a music teacher, remained in St. Paul, and as soon as an opportunity offered Sister Simeon was sent to Long Prairie. We can easily imagine how gladly she was wel-

comed by the two poor Sisters who had been so long and so anxiously expecting her. Additions for schoolrooms and other purposes
had been built to the old storehouse, making their dwelling place
much more commodious than at first; now that there were three
Sisters, they considered themselves quite a community.

During the winter Sister Scholastica began to feel the effects of
the cold and the many privations of the mission; her health was evidently failing. She had never been very strong, and the fear of losing
so useful a member induced Mother Celestine to make a change.
Sister Cesarine was accordingly given charge of the community and
Sister Scholastica returned to St. Paul, February, 1854. She was
accompanied by Sister Simeon, whom, as she was yet a novice,
Mother Seraphine was anxious to keep near her until after her pro-
fession. In January, 1854, a few weeks previous to the departure of
Mother Scholastica, Sister Ursula arrived at Long Prairie.

In those early days when all were pioneers in Minnesota, accommodations for travel were neither so expeditious, nor so comfortable
as they are now. Trips were never taken either for pleasure or for
health; it was absolute necessity alone that obliged one to undertake
a journey.

Long Prairie is over a hundred miles from St. Paul. This distance
had to be made in open wagons over very rough roads. The wagons
were always heavily laden with supplies for the agency. It usually
took four days to go from St. Paul to Long Prairie.

Sister Ursula relates the following particulars of her first trip to
the wild woods: "The teams from the reservation were down for their
New Year's supply of merchandise, early in January they were to
return, and I was to go on one of them. How well I remember the
appearance of the vehicle, as, loaded with barrels and boxes and
bags of various sizes, it drove up in front of the convent for poor little me. (Sister was very small). I was, as we supposed, very comfort-
ably wrapped up, and as I climbed to my place among the sundries
of the load I felt that myself and civilization were parting forever.
The drivers were two young half-breeds, who could speak very little
English. As I spoke neither French nor Indian, I could obtain no
information about the country through which we were journeying. I
knew I was traveling in obedience to those who had a right to command, and I resigned myself to the guidance of Divine Providence,
speaking little, but thinking much.

"The first night we lodged at a farm house occupied by an old couple and their son. The old lady was quite charmed with me, and tried
by every possible persuasion to induce me to remain with her. The
next morning I again clambered to my position behind the drivers,

and with the cheering prospect of another long cold day's journey before me we started. About noon we were overtaken by a team going to the pineries with a supply of provisions for the lumbermen. The driver, whose name I afterwards learned was Moran, appeared anxious to keep us in sight when we halted for the night; he questioned me as to where I was going, why I was alone, etc. He told me he was going beyond Long Prairie, and urged me to take a seat in his wagon, declaring in terms more emphatic than elegant, that the half-breeds did not take care of me, and that I would never reach the mission alive.

The weather was very cold; the drivers with the instinct of self-preservation peculiar to their race, had appropriated the extra blankets and buffalo robes sent with us. I had suffered intensely the day before; so when Mr. Moran assured me that the two teams would travel in company, I accepted his courtesy. During the remainder of my trip I was well cared for; at night the best accommodations were always secured for me. My comfort and how he could add to it, seemed to be his one thought; no father could have been more thoughtfully kind. When I arrived safely at the end of my journey, I was greatly surprised to hear that Mr. Moran was a most staunch Orangeman. I have never met him since, but I often pray for him."

In May, 1854, Sister Gregory was sent to Long Prairie. She was a young Canadian novice who could speak no English. The Sisters who were there could not speak the French, and Sister Gregory was very lonesome. Her reminiscences of the place are not pleasant. She was afraid of the Indians, and they were not slow to perceive it. She was necessarily often alone in the house, when the other Sisters were visiting the sick or attending to the distribution of the supplies; on these occasions the Indian children generally managed to raise some disturbance for the avowed purpose of terrifying her. Snakes were another cause of great annoyance to Sister Gregory. They were very numerous and were constantly crawling into the house. It appears from what she says that they were very fond of music; whenever anyone played on the organ, the snakes would come crawling in, stretch themselves out on the floor, and remain quiet, with their heads poised in the air, as though they were listening most attentively. This performance seemed to be a source of much amusement to the Father who was delighted to play for so charmed an audience.

Sister Gregory, after she had been there a few weeks, felt convinced that she had no vocation for the conversion of the Indians. Father Fisher, who was then in charge of the mission, could not speak French, and as there was no other person there who could understand her, she had recourse to God. The apartment in which the Blessed Sacrament was reserved was very small, and Sister thought her prayers would be the sooner heard if offered in "God's great temple, the silent groves." She, therefore, selected a dense grove of oak trees near the house, and every day she would repair to the place and offer up her fervent prayers for guidance and deliverance. She had a great devotion to St. Francis Xavier, and she most earnestly implored his intercession. Her prayers were heard and answered, for after having spent there only three months, which were months of great trial to her, she was summoned home to St. Paul.

Sister Simeon again returned to her dear Indians in September, and remained there until the mission was finally closed in 1855.

The Sisters had nothing to do with the closing of the Long Prairie mission where great hardship had to be borne and sacrifices made. The Sisters were devoted to their work. They were sorry to leave the little ones whom they had learned to love for God's own dear sake.

The temporal affairs were in the hands of the superintendent who managed things badly and involved the mission in debt. As the funds used belonged to the government, the Bishop had to suffer the consequences. He was much grieved at the thought of taking the Sisters away from the Indians for whose instruction he was so anxious; but as the St. Paul and the St. Anthony foundations were increasing, and the demand for Sisters in both places begin greater than the supply, he reluctantly concluded to withdraw the Sisters.

In May, 1855, when the Indians were removed to Blue Earth, Sisters Cesarine, Ursula and Simeon came home to St. Paul. This closed the first Indian mission in Minnesota."

We get another look at the travails of early missionaries to the Native Americans by returning to John Johnson's (Enmegahbowh) letters to Nathan Richardson of Little Falls. You will recall from Chapter IV that Johnson was an Ottawa Indian who served so faithfully as deacon of the Episcopal St. Columba Mission on Gull Lake. In his letters to Judge Richardson he describes his journey to the new reservation for the Ojibwe at White Earth (near Mahnomen) and his work there. He left Gull Lake after Hole-in-the-Day II burned his church down and threatened to kill him for alerting the Whites at the Indian Agency that they were about to be attacked. You will recall that the vast majority of Pillager Ojibwe from Crow Wing and Gull Lake moved to White Earth over the objections of Hole-in-the-Day who chose to stay behind after nearly all of his people had deserted him. Enmegahbow (Johnson) apparently left with the last contingent. The narrative which follows begins with his journey. The fact many of the Ojibwe at White Earth were not from Gull Lake or Crow Wing added to his anxieties.

> *These chiefs and warriors were all heathen. They worshipped to wood and stone. They* go to meet a man who comes with a different religious spirit, a man who comes to destroy and annihilate their religious faith and worship, the grand medicine faith of our forefathers and great grandfathers. This man, Enmegahbowh came to teach them a new religion. (Some of these chiefs had heard my teaching before they were removed). What changed them, and caused they to grasp the Christian teachings?*

First Episcopal Convert at Gull Lake, 1852. Rev. J. Lloyd Breck at the right and Rev. En-me-gah-bowh (John Johnson) at the left.

> *The first night of our encampment shall never be forgotten. We were talking and talking about our future, what to do and how to live in the new country, White Earth. I was so glad to hear them. I did not at once urge upon them that they all must turn to Christianity. This very point I leave until I know the favorable time has arrived. Our encampment four nights were spent talking of our great aim to raise them from their present condition. On the fourth day all left me to go home and bear the message that the poor Enmegahbowh*

*Apparently Johnson was met by a delegation from White Earth who were aware of his coming.

was coming sure, and would be there in two days. And this made no little stir with gladness. But there was one, an educated mixed blood, who was opposed to my coming, and he told the heathen that I was coming to do much injury to them and to their new country. The chiefs and warriors gave no heed, and his foolish talking did not amount to much of anything.

I arrived on Friday. A little comfortable log house had been provided for my dwelling house. Sunday came, and to my great astonishment, chiefs and headmen, women and children, of all grades, came to listen to my teachings. I was moved with compassion to see them seek shelter and strong stockade for shelter, the most impregnable fortress of Christian religion, the only hope of salvation for my unfortunate race.

My greatest aim was to catch all the leading chiefs and to kill all their little hope that was in them, because when this is done and accomplished, I shall think that my work is truly commenced. This had truly come to pass. I have never seen so much earnestness manifested by these chiefs, talking and talking to their people to receive my instructions, the only hope of our people and of their welfare.

During the winter we used the largest wigwam or log house, and during the summer I held my public services under the shade of the trees. In the second year I had nearly all the chiefs and the leading men and women and children under my teachings. I must say I have lived with my own people from the beginning of my days to the present time. I never saw so large a community of heathen people live in so harmoniously and in so great peace. It was like one family. O, those early days of yore! I long to see and enjoy their blessings. At that early day we had no Devil spirit nor anything to make us dumb and crazy. We loved and helped one another. I have often remarked to my wife that I was in a new world, and with new human beings. My joy was full, and I had plenty to give away to others. Thus, my dear Mr. Richardson, the whole work moved on harmoniously and in great peace, for there was nothing to interrupt nor impede our enterprises until the Devil spirit entered into our peaceful abodes. Drunkenness put on all their garb, and beautiful she pretended to be, but she soon demolished and impeded our whole work. The various species of human beings began to arrive and our efforts began to slacken and be impeded. Before this I had the biggest chieftain under my instruction. As I have remarked already the head chief, White Cloud, came to my house and said, "Enmegahbowh, my brother-in-law, I came to make known what is in my heart. We are very near the country of our great enemies, the Sioux nation. Several months ago the Pillager Indians went over not very far from us, and killed a *whole family and scalped them. I shall expect them to make retaliation of perhaps they are preparing to make a great war against us. Several of us chiefs and head warriors propose to go to the Sioux country to try to make peace with them, and on reaching their country we will leave our guns behind us and go to grasp their hands without any war implements about us. The great enemies, seeing us without arms shall be fully convinced that our hearts are fully prepared to make peace, a permanent peace, not for one month or year; but for all time to come. I know it is a great risk and a great venture of faith. Now, dear brother-in-law, why should I propose this great undertaking, a dangerous and uncertain path for reaching the object sought for? My heart has been greatly changed from deep-seated hatred to loving my enemies. My fathers and myself even, have worshipped to the Unknown God, yes, even to wood and stone. Today my people have turned their hearts to the living God and are worshipping Him. I hope with true hearts. It is under His great protection I propose to visit my enemies. I am confident to reach the lands of my enemies without anything happening to me. God is my hope and my trust and I shall go with these staffs."*

I said, "Now my dear friend, it is a great risk and a great undertaking and the words you have spoken are the true armor and are worth more than one hundred of the best warriors. Yes, God knows that we have been wandering through the various ways, here and there, without God and without hope in the world. Our country was taken away from you. You became shipwrecked like an orphan without a father to guide and protect you, and finally you were moved away from your bondage of sin and misery to seek a far country, and through your wanderings you have at last found a country. White Earth, where honey and milk flow. Here you are almost bewildered, and at last begin a new life in a new country. The poor Enmegahbowh arrived. He commenced to give you instruction and said to you all, my friends, please let me tell you what is true, and then invited you, saying, why halt ye between two opinions? If the Great God be God, serve him, or if Baal be God, serve him. Dear friends, you have heeded it, and taken my instructions, and have become true worshipers of the true and living God. Yes, dear friends go, go! God, whom you have trusted and worshipped, will guide and protect you to accomplish the great work; and peace and harmony shall be perpetuated all the days of your lives."

Again he said, "I shall be gone ten days. In ten days I shall be back to see you all again if nothing happens to me."

On the following day the chiefs with their warriors started away to the country of their great enemies. Nine days passed away and tomorrow was the day appointed for their return home. During the eighth night hardly anyone slept to await the ninth day. The ninth day came. My people, both men and women, stirred together. Here and there a group of men and women were standing toward afternoon. No appearance of our men was seen. Late in the night the men and women retired to their home, and on the next day the men and women again appeared on the same watch ground where they were waiting yesterday. Again they were disappointed as they were yesterday. No one came. Toward the evening the people began to feel uneasy about their friends. On the third day when no friend appeared, they became hopeless and despaired. They thought their friends must have been killed surely. On the fourth day my people came in to ask me what I thought about our friends. I said with a confident tone, in my great faith, "My friends, do not become hopeless. I know that they are all still living, and we shall soon see them coming home all safe, I say this, the Great Spirit will not forsake them in time of their danger. He knows them, and they trusted in Him. And besides, their work is great, and He will assist them to do it and to accomplish it." This talk relieved them greatly and on the fifth day some one took a walk a long distance toward the road our friends took when they started away from us. He brought the word that he heard guns fired a long distance away toward the path our friends took.

The news soon spread to the whole settlement, and the people began to gather waiting for someone to arrive. In about three hours our friends appeared upon a hill and began to fire their guns. Men and women, even children ran toward them, to shake hands with them, singing the song of peace for what they have accomplished. Here was large gathering of men, women and children. The friends came and shook hands with me heartily, and with much joy and peace.

Thus, Hon. N. Richardson, you can see and understand what the Christian Indian had accomplished, a permanent peace and forever.

John Johnson was evidentially more successful in converting Native Americans to Christianity than were most white missionaries. This seems to have been true in other parts of the country as well. Johnson was ordained an Episcopal priest while serving at White Earth.

Born in Austria, Father Pierz was one of the more successful white ministers who worked with the American Indians. We will discuss his ministry further in Chapter IX. We have already told of the important role he played in persuading his friend Hole-in-the-Day II to sign a peace agreement with the State of Minnesota. Before coming to

Minnesota, Father Pierz had a successful ministry among the Ottawa in Michigan. Because of his reputation, Bishop Cretin recruited him to work among the Pillagers with headquarters at Crow Wing. It was in his church yard that Chief Hole-in-the-Day II was buried.

Father Pierz also had a ministry to a small group of Whites at Belle Plain, just north of Little Falls. Energetic as he was, he also established a Pillager congregation on Mille Lacs Lake; he started to build a church there but ran out of funds. He traveled widely throughout Northern Minnesota.

Thus we have seen struggling but often successful missionary efforts among the Winnnebago and Ojibwe Indians of Central Minnesota. It is significant that these were the first organized efforts in what became Minnesota. Father Hennepin's short stay at Mille Lacs Lake and Father Alneau's brief ministry as Pierre La Verendrye's priest in residence at Fort St. Charles on the Northwest Angle of the Lake of the Woods both preceded the Winnebago missions but they were not sustained, organized efforts.

CHAPTER VIII

The Red River
Woods Ox Cart Trail

Were it not for the blessing of Hole-in-the-Day the elder and the help of his men, the critically important and historic Woods Trail may never have been built, and were it not for Hole-in-the-Day the Younger and his men, parts of it may never have been shortened and improved. But let us go back to the beginning, and talk about why there was a need for ox cart trails (there were three of them) and why these important links between St. Paul and what is now the Winnipeg region were created.

It all began with Lord Selkirk (Thomas Douglas) the English Peer who was the majority owner of the Hudsons Bay Company in the early 1800s. He had a vision for what is now southern Manitoba, including Winnipeg, and that was to establish a farming community. The land was open and easily cultivated (mostly prairie) and yet there were plenty of trees in the area for fuel and constructing buildings.

The area was remote—hundreds of miles from eastern Canadian population centers-but it was accessible from three different directions:
1) There was access from the north via Hudsons Bay (the head-quarters of Selkirk's company) by way of the Nelson River and Lake Winnipeg.
2) There was access from the south by way of the Minnesota River, Lake Traverse and the Red River.
3) And there was access from the east via the Great Lakes, the Boundary Waters, the Winnipeg River and Lake Winnipeg.

In 1812, Lord Selkirk brought in potential farmers from several different European countries (especially Switzerland) and called his new country "Assinaboia", named for the tribe of Sioux* who inhabited the area. This first settlement was doomed to failure. For one thing, even though there was access from three directions, the area was so remote it was difficult to bring in livestock and to market the crops that were

*Although the Assinaboin were a Sioux tribe, they usually allied themselves with the Algonquin tribes: the Cree, Monsonis and Ojibwe. They had been chased out of what is now Wisconsin by other Sioux tribes. They fled north into what is now Manitoba. "Assinaboin" means "Snakes of the rocks".

produced. The more serious and immediate problem, however, was the arch enemy and fur trading rival, the Northwest Company. The latter did not want their competition to have a permanent settlement in such a strategic location. When Assinaboia was just three years old, the agents of the Northwest Company, many of them Indians (some came from as far away as Leech Lake), burned out the community and killed all the inhabitants. They then established their own headquarters there and built a fort. The next year, Selkirk brought in a small army, including Ojibwe from the Lake of the Woods. The leader of the Lake of the Woods Indians was John Tanner, a white man raised by Indians.*

Thomas Douglas, Earl of Selkirk

They not only captured this fort but also other Northwest outposts. Lord Selkirk then re-established his colony on the Red River.

The bloody rivalry of the two giant fur trading companies continued a few more years but the conflict hurt both so badly they finally had the wisdom to merge in 1821. Actually, it was more of a takeover by the Hudsons Bay Company—which remains in operation in Canada to this day.

Hardly luxury travel. Note the mud-covered wheels.

John Tanner (his Indian name was "the Falcon") is the hero of a book by this author, entitled "White Indian Boy".

The carts usually had a tarp to protect the cargo during indecent weather.

The new Red River settlement did survive, but growth was slow and painful. Meanwhile, a group of Metis (mixed bloods) began settling around a trading post at the mouth of the Pembina River. They were the offspring of white traders, who had been in the general vicinity for nearly one hundred years, and their Indian wives.

As the population grew in the Red River Valley from Pembina to Lake Winnipeg, they found their best opportunity to obtain supplies and for trade in general was to the south via the Red and Minnesota Rivers. Their major linkage was with Fort Snelling and the fledgling village of St. Paul (first called "Pigs Eye").

Water travel was seasonal and the route was long and indirect, and thus the ox carts came into use. The vehicles were actually invented by the French in eastern Canada. It is said that the first carts had wheels made of the cross-sections of large trees. These were replaced with spokes and rims. The Metis were the first in the valley to use the improved carts and by 1820 there were caravans of carts heading west across the prairies to bring back the fruits of buffalo hunts.

The two wheel carts were drawn by an ox or a horse and could carry more than four or five pack animals. They were made entirely of wood, which had both advantages and drawbacks. The wood construction meant that all too often they would break down on the rough terrain, but with trees usually nearby new parts could be fashioned. The wooden hubs revolved around ungreased wooden axles, causing a continuous squeal that could sometimes be heard for more than a mile. The carts could be disassembled and floated across deeper streams with the cargo intact. The wheels were large – about five feet in diameter – which meant they were less likely to be stuck in the mud. Perhaps they can best be described as "practical." They proved to be the best linkage between the northern Red River Valley and St. Paul for nearly fifty years.

Turning a cart into a boat.

There were three major Red River Ox Cart trails:
1) The Minnesota River Trail
2) The Middle Trail, which was mostly a prairie trail that reached the Mississippi River at St. Cloud and
3) The North or Woods Trail which crossed the prairies to Ottertail and Leaf Lakes and then followed the Leaf, Crow Wing and Mississippi Rivers to Fort Snelling and St. Paul. As it passed through the Crow Wing watershed it added another piece of important history to our area of focus.

The choice of trails depended on the time of the year, the amount of snow or rainfall and, perhaps most importantly, on the chances of attack by the Sioux. Our Woods or North trail ran through Ojibwe country, and the members of this tribe were usually friendly and often helpful.

The ox cart trails were more than routes of commerce. They were also a route of escape for dissatisfied residents of Lord Selkirk's colony. As we have already mentioned, the remote location made it difficult to secure supplies or market produce. Winter weather was often severe and spring floods were frequently a serious problem. The more hospitable climate to the south was tempting. The first migration out of the valley was in 1821, when five families successfully reached Fort Snelling. Two years later, a Scottish family (David Tully) started south but all were killed by a band of Sioux (probably Lakota) near present day Grand Forks. Later, that same year (1823) a group of thirteen Swiss and German families were successful in reaching St. Paul. They were well armed and followed the Red River—Minnesota River route.

In the spring of 1823, after a winter of deep snow, there was a devastating flood. This was the "last straw" for the remaining Swiss settlers. Joined by a few Scottish, Irish and French Canadians, nearly 300 disenchanted souls headed south. The Swiss did not stop at Fort Snelling, but went on to Galena, Illinois, where they were already other Swiss settlers. All their worldly goods were in carts drawn by either an ox or a horse.

The migration continued into the 1840s, but the Selkirk colony actually grew in spite of the large numbers leaving. By 1834 there were about 2,600 inhabitants in the northern Red River valley. In addition, about 400 of the Metis left Pembina and traveled north to settle on the Assinaboin River. They had learned (in 1823) that they had been living south of the 49th parallel and were therefore in the United States. They chose to remain Canadians. Starting in the 1830s, the trails were used more for commerce than for migration.

The Woods Trail, unlike the first two, started at Fort Snelling and was developed north to the Selkirk colony. A man named Peter Garrioch, along with his crew, had traveled down one of the other trails to Fort Snelling, but was warned that the Sioux were "on the warpath" and that the two prairie trails would not be safe. He was determined to reach home before winter set in and knew he had no other choice than to cut a trail through the woodlands where the friendly Ojibwe were in control. They left Fort Snelling in the early autumn of 1844. They had little difficulty following the established trail along the Mississippi to the village of Crow Wing, but from there on travel was far different. They had to cut a new trail through huge pines, many of which had fallen from old age or because of wind storms, through wet swamps and across several rivers and streams. It seems from his account that they were carrying a large amount of cargo in their ox carts and therefore, couldn't get by with just any old narrow walking trail; they had to build a road.

Garrioch gave much credit to the Ojibwe for keeping them from getting lost and for helping them find the best route. Hole-in-the-Day the Elder was ruling Central Minnesota at the time, but there is no mention of him. We can be quite certain, however, that the Ojibwe men would never have guided Garrioch's crew without the chief's blessing. The Indians were far more than guides; they helped with the actual construction. It was November when they finally reached Detroit Lake. Beyond Detroit Lake lay the prairies and familiar ground, so the Pillagers were no longer needed. By now the weather had turned bitter cold and they were confronted with drifting snow. Yet, they made it home. The colonists listened to Garrioch's tales of troubles, but were nevertheless happy that there was now an alternate route through Ojibwe country. The very next spring the new trail was put to good use as a caravan of about 80 carts followed the new Woods Trail south. With the Sioux becoming more hostile, this became the route of choice.

Traveling from north to south, the majority of the trail was over prairie and along easily traveled glacial ridges. It did not hit woodlands until it reached Detroit Lake, which was first called "Lake 44" because that was the year in which the trail was created. From here, the trail entered the forest, working its way through present day cities of Frazee and Perham, along present Highway U.S. 10, the Leaf Hills, old Ottertail City (an important trading post but only a few houses), Leaf City (actually one house between the two Leaf Lakes), Wadena (Sunnybrook Park), Old Wadena (on the Crow Wing River), across the Crow Wing, and then followed the north side of that river to the community of Crow Wing across the Mississippi. The trail then followed the Mississippi to Fort Snelling. The portion of the route between Leaf Lakes and Old Crow Wing was considered the most difficult because of the swamps, thick forests and difficult river crossings. When the trail first opened in 1844, the villages of Crow Wing and Ottertail City were in existence. Old Wadena came into being later, because of the new trail. Oxen were used more on the Woods Trail than horses, for the reason that when they stepped on soft or swampy ground their cloven hoofs would spread out and keep them from becoming mired.

The Woods Trail saw a lot of history. It was there during the last years of Hole-in-the-Day the Elder's reign, during all of Hole-in-the-Day the Younger's years in power, during the time the Winnebago Reservation was headquartered at Long Prairie; and part of this route was used by the Gull Lake—Crow Wing—Mississippi Pillagers as they traveled to their new reservation at White Earth (near present day Mahnomen). The Gull—Crow Wing Indian Agency was also located on the Woods Trail.

Today, parts of the trail have become country roads or even highways, such as U.S. 10. Here and there portions of the old trail are still visible. There are arguments among locals as to exactly where the trail ran and where it crossed rivers and streams. Part of the confusion is because the route would change depending on the weather or even fires. High water in streams or spring floods would cause the travelers to seek new crossings. Spring ice-outs could change the depth of streams; fast-moving ice chunks could dig new holes or fill up old holes with sand. As the area became settled, smaller trails would head off the main trail, causing further confusion today.

We know that the Woods Trail crossed the Crow Wing at Old Wadena. After crossing the Crow Wing, the trail followed the north side of the river until it reached the village of Crow Wing—which lay across the Mississippi. But there is a trail on the south bank of the Crow Wing, starting at McGivern Park where it may have crossed the river. Going west from the park, there are remnants still visible—including a short

Source: "Pages in History", Verndale Centennial Book – 1883-1893.

A depression in the landscape marks the trail where it came down the hill at Old Wadena.

segment in the author's backyard. Fifty years ago, what is now 130th Street along the south bank of the Crow Wing River, was referred to as "the Cart Trail." Early Staples area residents claimed this cart trail was a shortcut to Ottertail and the Leaf Lakes.

During the 1850s, attempts were made to improve the Woods Trail. Congress approved a plan to improve the 125 miles stretch from Crow Wing to the Wild Rice River. A feasibility study was made by E.A. Holmes; he reported that it would take a lot more than just cutting trees to straighten the road and to make it more easily traveled. In 1857, Congress approved a more modest effort to improve the trail from Crow Wing to Old Wadena (37 miles). It was a tough job and they gave up eight miles short of their goal when they hit a big swamp west of present day Staples and ran out of money.

Chief Hole-in-the-Day II grew tired of waiting for the promised improvement of the trail and improved and shortened (straightened out) the road between Crow Wing and Fort Ripley, using his own men and resources. He also paid for the construction of a new ferry for use across the Mississippi at Crow Wing.

The Woods Trail played an important role in 1858 in an effort to improve commerce between St. Paul and the Canadian portion of the Red River Valley. The St. Paul Chamber of Commerce offered a reward of $2,000* to anyone who could initiate steamboat service on the Red

*According to some reports the amount of the reward was larger.

River. Anson Northup won the prize. He had operated a steamboat between Little Falls and Aitkin. That winter, he and his men dismantled the boat at Crow Wing and fashioned a new hull. Northup named the boat for himself. While it was still winter, a crew of about 60 men with 34 teams of horses carried the parts via the Woods Trail all the way to the Red River. There, they re-assembled it and steamed down the Red River to Fort Garry (now Winnipeg). The next year, Northup collected the reward and promptly sold his boat to a stagecoach company which then used the boat for several years to transport its coach passengers to and from the Canadian settlements in the northern part of the valley.

The "Anson Northup," first steamboat on the Red River. It was hauled in pieces in the winter over the Woods Trail.

Courtesy Crow Wing County Historical Society

CHAPTER IX

Old Wadena and Old Crow Wing

Both of these communities were in existence during the times of the Hole-in-the-Days and both were important to the development of what is now Minnesota in the 1800s. Today they are truly "ghost towns."

Old Wadena and Old Crow Wing were heavily impacted by the Woods Red River Cart Trail. In the case of Wadena, the community probably would never have existed without the trail. Crow Wing, on the other hand, was in existence as a fur trading post long before the creation of the trail in 1844, but the coming of the carts contributed significantly to its emergence as the commercial and political center of Northern Minnesota.

Both communities held great promise, and both died for reasons beyond their control.

OLD WADENA

"Wadena" is Ojibwe for "little round hill", and there is a hill that fits that description on the site. In fact, there are several hills in the vicinity and J.V. Brower, an amateur explorer and archeologist in the last half of the 1800s, thought the name could have referred to the several hills, not just the one. There is one other theory as to how the village got its name; it has been suggested that it was named for Chief Wadena, son of Chief Bad Boy who lived on Gull Lake and later on Mille Lacs.

From Lord Selkirk's colony in Manitoba to Fort Snelling is a long journey. The approximately 350 mile trip by ox or horse drawn cart took about a month using the Woods Trail. Actually, the time could vary considerably because the terrain would change with the seasons or because of storms, floods or fires. When the trail was created in 1844, there were already trading posts at Old Crow Wing, Leaf Lakes and Ottertail. They were logical places to acquire supplies, make repairs or just rest. But there was no such place between Crow Wing and the western posts, this was a journey of nearly 100 miles and took five or six days. There was a need for another stop-over place. Old Wadena became that place. But why here? Why Wadena?

There are a couple of reasons: first, the trail followed the Leaf River and this is where that river entered the Crow Wing, and secondly, this was one of the better places to ford the Crow Wing River. The river bottom (and therefore depth) could change from year to year. As the ice went out each spring it could gouge out deep holes or fill them in. Water levels would also vary by the season. This may be the reason there is debate to this day as to the exact spot the trail crossed the river. We do know that the crossing at the village site wasn't always all that easy because a rope ferry was created. Since the ferry was created after the village became a reality, it is likely that its purpose was to serve villagers living on both sides of the river and may not have been the actual cart crossing.

Our knowledge of Old Wadena is really quite limited. We know there was a general store that was reportedly well stocked to meet the needs of the travelers. Peter Roy operated an inn of sorts that he called the "Half Way House", so named because of its location between Ottertail and Old Crow Wing. The users of the trail spent most nights under the stars, but for the more affluent, the inn provided an opportunity for sleeping under a roof in a real bed. As mentioned earlier, Roy was a Federal Interpreter and a member of the Minnesota Territorial Legislature. We also found him traveling with Chief Bad Boy to visit Chief Hole-in-the-Day in the hope of persuading him to not kill the Whites he held captive.

August Aspinwall was the visionary who actually founded Wadena and did the most to build the community. He was only there between 1856 and 1858, but during that time he:

- persuaded the Territorial Legislature to create a new county (Old Wadena had been in Cass County) named for his new community;
- persuaded the legislature to make (Old) Wadena the county seat;
- along with a man named George Valenberg, persuaded the legislature to authorize a rope ferry across the Crow Wing River;
- filed a plat of the town site (1857) between the Partridge River and the Leaf River, on both sides of the Crow Wing; his brother, Nathaniel, was a civil engineer and he laid out the town site;
- Designated a town square on the west bank and
- helped (Old) Wadena to qualify for a post office and had himself appointed postmaster.

During the peak years (1855-1860) hundreds of travelers used the Woods Trail and Wadena grew accordingly – on both sides of the Crow Wing River. Houses were built, streets were platted and families moved in. Warren Upham in his book entitled "Minnesota Geographic Place Names", listed Wadena as a town of approximately 100 population. All other sources give a considerably smaller figure. Peter Roy, the inn keeper, took an unofficial census in 1857 in preparation for statehood the next year, and reported a population of just 19 people in four residences. J.V. Brower found only seven people living in Old Wadena in 1863, but said that the peak years ended in 1860.

The plat for the village of Wadena was registered in St. Cloud. It shows that Nathaniel Aspinwall was truly a professional. The community was surveyed in blocks and 60 foot lots. The streets, which paralleled the Crow Wing River, were 80 feet wide; the avenues were 60 feet wide. All were named. The avenues were numbered and the streets had names like "Vine", "Carthage" and "Venus." It is interesting that a town square was also included in the design. Nathaniel plotted two other communities for brother August: "Detroit" at Detroit Lakes and "Elmira" at the outlet of Rush Lake. Both were on the portion of the Woods Trail often called the "Crow Wing—Ottertail Road."

Aspinwall had envisioned a booming community and hoped to profit from the sale of the land. He did sell ten lots to John Beaumont of Freeport, Illinois, for $500, a whole block to Dorilla Barnes for one dollar and 44 blocks to the Ike Moultons for one dollar. The last couple sold the land later for $8,000!

During the development of Wadena, Aspinwall also ran a sawmill at the mouth of Gull River. It is probably safe to assume that much of the lumber used in his buildings came from there.

Aspinwall's main building has been variously described as an inn, a trading post, a store and a home. The building that housed Peter Roy's various enterprises has been described in much the same way. Roy and Aspinwall were friends and sometimes partners. The descriptions may very well be for the same building, but we don't know for sure; they may have been separate enterprises.

In 1858, August Aspinwall moved on, sometimes running sawmills, sometimes operating trading posts, often involved in real estate speculation (including Aitkin and Grand Rapids), always eager for new ventures. His speculations usually involved his brother Nathaniel and a second brother, Edward, who receives little mention.

The Panic of 1887 had a long lasting effect on the economy and made it doubly hard for the Aspinwalls to succeed in their various business attempts. Nathaniel finally gave up and returned to the family home in Elmira, New York, where he subsequently joined the U.S. Cavalry.

The Woods Trail eventually fell into disuse because the reason it was created was no longer a concern. Following the Sioux Uprising in 1862, that tribe was driven out of Minnesota; they were no longer a threat to travelers on the two more southerly trails. Old Wadena might still have survived and become the "Verndale" or "Staples" of that area, but the Northern Pacific Railroad was constructed a few miles south of the community in 1872. Staples became an important Division Point. This meant that train crews would change here and it would also be a place where equipment would be serviced.

The Old Wadena site shall remain historic for two other very important reasons. It was here, at the mouth of the Partridge River in the early 1780s, that the French Trader known as "the Blacksmith" had his post, which was attacked by a large band of Sioux (page 19) and it was on the Leaf River, near its mouth, where John Cadotte had his trading post in 1792 and had his own troubles with his Sioux neighbors (page 22).

Today, the wilderness has reclaimed its own and little evidence remains of the once thriving community. The name, however, has survived and has been claimed by the important county seat town 15 miles to the west and it is also the name of the county.

Efforts are currently underway to mark each historic site, expand the potential as a campground and meeting place and to eventually do some actual restoration. On organization known as WHELP (Wadena Historical Environmental and Learning Program) is spearheading the effort.

Archaeologist Doug Birk has been exploring the Old Wadena site. His findings confirm the Euro American presence, probably starting in 1857, and continuing an undetermined number of years. Artifacts supporting this finding include the charred wall of a building, machine-made square nails, part of the stem of a pipe, an axe head, bottle or chimney glass shards, shell buttons, cloth fragments, a buckle, pieces of coal, etc. Birk also found evidence of much earlier Native American cultures including shards or "shardlets" of ancient Indian pottery and particles of stone shaved in the manufacture of weapons and tools.

OLD CROW WING

The village of Crow Wing took its name from the river that enters the Mississippi across from the village site. The Ojibwe had given the river its name; in their language it was "Kah-kah-gi-wi-giwan-isepi". They had so named it because the river flowed into the Mississippi with a sweep that resembled a raven's wing. It is also possible that it received its name from the shape of the island at the mouth of the river. The French had no name for ravens; to them, all big black birds were crows;

hence, it became the Crow Wing River.

The village of Crow Wing was also the victim of the Northern Pacific Railroad. That company literally created the town of Brainerd when it crossed the Mississippi eight miles to the north. If it were not for Crow Wing State Park, only a few depressions in the earth would mark the site of one of the most important communities in the Territory of (and later State of) Minnesota.

In its prime, Crow Wing boasted stores, warehouses, blacksmith shops, an inn, three churches (Catholic, Episcopal and Lutheran), dozens of homes and at one time seven bars or liquor stores. It had the first school in Crow Wing County (1849) and was named the

William W. Warren, resident of Old Crow Wing, member of the Territorial Legislature, author of "A History of the Ojibways" and self-ordained Christian missionary to his people.

temporary seat of that county in 1857. It became important politically. At one time it was home to two members of the 18 member Minnesota Territorial Legislature. There were Jeremiah Russell and Allan Morrison.

Crow Wing village in 1859 as pictured in Harpers magazine

William Warren, the author, had been a member of the Territorial Legislature earlier.

Both Chiefs Hole-in-the-Day had homes here. Major Cullen, the local Indian Agent, described the home of Hole-in-the-Day II to the St. Paul Pioneer and Democrat thus:

First School District No. 1 – Crow Wing County

Chief Hole-in-the-Day has built himself a gay old house on his reserved 640 acres at Crow Wing on the Mississippi River. The house has cost him $6,000 in gold and is nearly surrounded by a piazza. The chief is living with six wives in all the splendor of a Mormon Bishop. His parlor is furnished with 17 rocking chairs, while the walls are hung with 8 large portraits, seven of which represent himself, and the other Major Cullen. They live like white folks, all sit at the same table and have the best china and coffee sets for every day use. He had over one hundred acres of his reserve under cultivation which brings forth bountifully. His wives work a large garden well stocked with flowers.

Since both Hole-in-the-Days were chiefs of the entire Gull Lake, Crow Wing and Mississippi bands of Ojibwe, it is logical that they had homes at more than one location; both also had homes at the east end of Gull Lake and the second Hole-in-the-Day had a farm on the Gull River – near its source.

Hole-in-the-Day II was buried in the Catholic Cemetery in Crow Wing following his assassination.

But let us get back to the beginning. The village of Crow Wing had its origin with the fur trade. The location made it a natural, located on the Mississippi across from the mouth of the Crow Wing River. As we said earlier, the Mississippi River was the major north-south route for the First Americans and the Crow Wing was often the preferred route when paddling north against the current. The Crow Wing River offered access to the Gull River, Gull Lake, Round Lake and then a whole series of short portages that gave access to Lakes like Winne, Leech, Sandy, Bemidji etc. Both routes passed Old Crow Wing.

We are not certain when the first Crow Wing trading post was built but James McGill had a winter post here in 1771. Jean Baptiste Perrault had a post here the winter of 1773. Allan Morrison, who was associated with the American Fur Company, recorded that he had a post on an island several miles north "of where Fort Ripley now stands" in 1823.

This may have been at the mouth of the Crow Wing River. We do know company records show that he moved the AFC headquarters from Fond du Lac to Crow Wing in that year. Morrison was probably the first permanent white resident of the village.

An aerial view of the wing-shaped island at the mouth of the Crow Wing. The arrow indicates where historian Carl Zappfe thought an early trading post may have been located. He thought it was Fort Duquesne; others think this particular fort was at the mouth of the Little Elk River.

Clement Beaulieu, another important trader, moved to Crow Wing about 1837. He stayed many years (until 1969) and later operated an inn and what was called a "dry goods store" in those days. He was part Ojibwe and part French and had the respect of both peoples. He had as much influence as anyone in persuading Hole-in-the-Day II to not kill the Whites he and his men had taken prisoner in the 1862 Uprising. When the Ojibwe were moved to the White Earth reservation (near Mahnomen) in 1869, Beaulieu went with them. Not surprisingly, he was soon back in business as a storekeeper!

Other traders associated with Crow Wing were U.S. Senator Henry Rice (whose rifle with his name inscribed on it was found in the river many years later), Paul Beaulieu and John Fairbanks. Another trader of note, Benjamin Baker (alias "Blue Beard") had a post two miles south of Crow Wing the winter of 1831-32.

From the time of the first trading posts (and probably much earlier) until 1868 when the Ojibwe were moved to White Earth, there were significant populations of American Indians in and around the community. Stanchfield, an early trader, reported approximately 500 Ojibwe in a village on an island at the mouth of the Crow Wing. It was no doubt a temporary village since the island floods most springs. At the time of the exodus to White Earth, some Ojibwe had been recent arrivals from Wisconsin. A significant number of "mixed bloods" were also living here at the time of the Exodus. Hole-in-the-Day II was opposed to the move to White Earth (although he had favored it earlier when he signed the treaty) but he especially objected to these newcomers moving to the new reservation.

Father Pierz

Courtesy Crow Wing County Historical Society

The village began to grow; by 1848 it had 37 permanent white residents and many more (but an unknown number) of American Indians. By 1870, the population of Whites had grown to about 200.

It is difficult to discern from census and other records the exact population of Crow Wing at any given time; however, the 1857 Crow Wing County census reported 32 dwellings and 176 white inhabitants. It is likely that most of them lived in and around the village. We do know, however, that there were some residents in other parts of Crow Wing County. For example, that same year a post office was established at Nokay, two miles north of Fort Ripley.

Crow Wing was the scene of fairly intensive missionary efforts. Father Pierz's first headquarters in Minnesota was located here in 1852. He had earned a reputation as an effective missionary to the American Indians from his twenty years of service to the Ottawa people of what is now Michigan. Bishop Cretin (of St. Paul) recruited Father Pierz and placed him "in complete charge of the Indian missions north of the Mississippi and to minister to white people living in the territory."

Father Pierz built his church in Crow Wing on a hill overlooking the village and the Mississippi River.* At this time the priest was over 50 years of age, but this did not slow him down. He also built a church to serve a small congregation of French Canadians at Belle Prairie in 1853 – a few miles north of Little Falls just off present highway 371. Pierz also evangelized the Ojibwe on Mille Lacs Lake and started the construction of a church there, but it was not finished for lack of funds. Father Pierz traveled widely, including visits to lakes as far north as Leech Lake and east to Fond du Lac and Grand Portage on Lake Superior. As stated in Chapter IV, the good priest had the respect and

Father Bulr built a new church in 1867.

friendship of Hole-in-the-Day II and he, along with Clem Beaulieu, Charles Sweet, Peter Roy and Chief Bad Boy convinced the chief not to kill the Whites his allies had taken captive (in 1862) but to sign a peace treaty with the State of Minnesota.

As mentioned previously, Chief Hole-in-the-Day, following his assassination, was buried in the Catholic cemetery in Crow Wing. A visitor to the village in 1871 reported seeing Hole-in-the-Day's grave. He described the burial plot as "10 by 20 with a wooden picket fence around it." Two of trader Morrison's children were buried in the same plot. The visitor said that there was a small wooden cross at the head of each grave.

Because of rumors that the chief's body had been removed and buried elsewhere (one story was that Hole-in-the-Day was re-buried under the flagpole in Pillager), in 1957, Russell Fridley, then Director of the Minnesota Historical Society, headed a party that excavated the grave. After all those years, there were few remains; not enough to prove anything.

There was also a Lutheran presence in Crow Wing. As mentioned in Chapter IV, Rev. Ron Ottomar Cloetter moved his mission to Crow Wing after his church on Lower Mission Lake – north of Brainerd – was burned down in 1862 by Hole-in-the-Day's men.

The economy of the village was helped significantly by the location of the Gull Indian agency only 6 miles up the Crow Wing River, just beyond the mouth of the Gull River and the location of Fort Ripley just 8 miles down the Mississippi. Crow Wing was located on the North Woods Ox Cart Trail. There was also a less used trail to Leech Lake.

The treaty of 1837* between the Ojibwe and the United States Government and signed by Hole-in-the-Day I (among others) included the right of lumber interests to log off a huge "upside down triangle" of land between the Mississippi and St. Croix Rivers. Stillwater was at the bottom point of the triangle and the village of Crow Wing was at the northwest corner. This, then, was the first area logged in what is now the State of Minnesota. It didn't take long to exhaust this timber supply. In ten years nearly all of the timber in the triangle had been harvested except the most northern portion. Operations did not reach Crow Wing at that time; they stopped temporarily at Mille Lacs Lake. In 1847 there was a need for a new treaty; this was signed by the younger Hole-in-the-Day. It covered another huge area including the Crow Wing River watershed, Gull River and Gull Lake and the nearby portion of the Mississippi. For this the chief received $1,000 a year in gold. By this treaty, the Crow Wing River and related territories became the second area logged in what became the State of Minnesota.

The village of Crow Wing prospered. The fur trade continued but it

*The Treaty of 1837 is printed in the appendix. Controversy continues to this day over whether or not special fishing and hunting rights guaranteed the Ojibwe are still in effect.

had begun to slow down. Henry Rice and a few other traders seized the opportunity. He built a sawmill at Little Falls but continued his operations at Crow Wing. Two mills were soon in operation in the vicinity of the village. From 1848 until its demise, Crow Wing was a logging town.

The cart trail, which had been extended west to Detroit Lake in 1844, received increasingly heavy traffic – the peak years being 1850 to 1860.

D.B. Herriman, who was appointed Indian Agent at the Gull River agency in 1853, credited Hole-in-the-Day with making major contributions to the development of the village of Crow Wing. The chief had been granted a section of land at the village site. He had a boat constructed, at his own expense that served as a ferry across the Mississippi. He also paid for the reconstruction of the trail between Crow Wing and Fort Ripley, shortening the distance by two miles. The chief boasted, "I am doing more by hard work for civilizing my tribe than any white man by the influence of money or government."

The demise of Old Crow Wing began with the removal of the Ojibwe population to White Earth (Mahnomen) in 1868. Two years before the exodus (1866), the local Indian Agent listed the Ojibwe population of the Gull Lake – Crow Wing – Mississippi and Mille Lacs area as 2,166. In the end, the Mille Lacs band did not have to leave (because they had stood up to Hole-in-the-Day in 1862), but nearly all of the remainder did leave. Even the mixed bloods and the late arrivers from Wisconsin moved to White Earth. Nevertheless, logging continued to thrive and with white settlers moving north, the business community continued to do well. In 1870, the village had a population of 200 of which 84 were children of school age, twenty-eight pupils attended a private school; the remainder were probably taught at home. The census listed 39 homes in the community.

The arrival of the Northern Pacific Railroad from the east and the creation of the town of Brainerd in 1870, where the railroad crossed the Mississippi, spelled the end of Old Crow Wing. The closing of Fort Ripley in 1877 didn't help either. In 1879, several buildings were destroyed by fire. During the next few years, houses and businesses were abandoned or moved – several to the place the Ojibwe called "New Town" (Brainerd).

The churches were closed and some of the dead in their cemeteries were exhumed and buried elsewhere – including Brainerd.

It was rumored after his death that Hole-in-the-Day had buried his gold on or near one of the several properties he owned. Many have sought the treasure, but as far as we know, if it even existed, it has never been found. The treaty settlements specified that both Hole-in-the-Days would personally receive payments in gold – not to mention monies paid to the tribe but channeled through the chiefs. Over the years, they could have accumulated considerable wealth; the rumors could be true!

CHAPTER X

White-Ojibwe Relations After The Hole-In-The-Days' Era

With the demise of Hole-in-the-Day II and the removal of most of the Pillagers headquartered around the Gull lake – Crow Wing Indian agency to the White Earth Reservation, relatively large numbers of white settlers began moving into the area. Occasionally Pillagers from the Leech Lake and upper Mississippi villages would visit the region, sometimes causing concern among the new Minnesotans. On the next page is a copy of a telegram originating in Motley in 1884, and addressed to Governor Hubbard demanding that Indians be removed from the vicinity of Motley. It is followed, however, by a letter from H. B. Morrison, owner of the Motley Brick and Lumber Co., denying any danger from the Pillagers.

BRAINERD'S BLEUBERRY WAR

The Blueberry War of 1872 brought a great deal of excitement to the frontier town. In July of that year, the twenty-year old daughter of David McArthur was sent on an errand to Crow Wing. When she did not return, a search party was organized. Although she was not found, rumors spread that two half-breeds had attacked and murdered her. Under interrogation, the suspects confessed and led authorities to a place where her body had been burned. They were promptly imprisoned in the local jail, a structure made of wood. A mob estimated at 300 people broke into the jail and took the prisoners to the Last Turn Saloon and prepared to hang them from a tall pine tree in front of the tavern. The first was quickly hung, but as the second was being "strung up", he freed his hands, grabbed the rope above his head, and scrambled up onto the branch over which the rope had been thrown. Several shots were fired from below and the half-breed was killed. People farther back in the crowd could not see what was happening and assumed Indians had come to the rescue. Most fled in pandemonium!

Still fearing Indian reprisals, soldiers were sent for; they arrived three days later by train.

Form No. 1.

THE WESTERN UNION TELEGRAPH COMPANY.

This Company TRANSMITS and DELIVERS messages only on conditions limiting its liability, which have been assented to by the sender of the following message.
Errors can be guarded against only by repeating a message back to the sending station for comparison, and the company will not hold itself liable for errors or delays in transmission or delivery of Unrepeated Messages, beyond the amount of tolls paid thereon, nor in any case where the claim is not presented in writing within sixty days after sending the message.
This is an UNREPEATED MESSAGE, and is delivered by request of the sender, under the conditions named above.
THOS. T. ECKERT, General Manager.   NORVIN GREEN, President.

NUMBER	SENT BY	REC'D, BY	CHECK		
My	n	6a	16 Paid / 19 9209		

Received: St Paul Minn   Aug 22   188[4]

Dated: Motley Minn 22

To: Governor Hubbard

Want Indians removed from vicinity
of Motley in forty eight
hours to save further trouble
answer

Many Citizens

OFFICE OF

H. B. MORRISON,

MANUFACTURER OF

BRICK AND LUMBER,

Motley, Minn. N.P.R.R. Aug. 22d 1884

Hon. S. Y. Jennison
St Paul Minn

Dear Sir:
Your favor of the 20th in
regard to Indians here is at hand
For my part I cannot see why
people here want their removal.
They came from Leech Lake and
are entirely harmless and industrious.
Five & six are at work for me and
some of them are working at the other
saw mill here.
The squaws are quite busily engaged
most of the time picking blue berries, and
recently have begun to bring in plums and
high bush cranberries.
Many of the Indians that have been here
the past month have gone back home

OFFICE OF

H. B. MORRISON,

MANUFACTURER OF

BRICK AND LUMBER,

Motley, Minn. N.P.R.R. _____ 1884

I am glad to have them here, as both mills
have had to rely on them for help since
harvest began,
I know of their doing no damage
to persons or property.
I hear that a telegram was sent from Motley
requesting their removal in forty eight
hours signed "Many Citizens". I am
told only two persons that had any
thing to do with the telegram and these
two are certainly not representative men
Yours truly
H. B. Morrison

TO THE CITIZENS OF MOTLEY, MINNESOTA
FROM THE MEN OF THE
47th INFANTRY DIVISION
MINNESOTA NATIONAL GUARD

Shortly thereafter, a fleet of Indian canoes was seen coming down the Mississippi. It was assumed the town was under attack. Actually, the canoes were filled with containers of blueberries which the Indians hoped to trade! The whole episode was given the name, the Blueberry War.

A BRIEF WHITE-OJIBWE CONFLICT NEAR ALDRICH IN 1874*

The Wadena County Historical Society provided the following account:

An unfortunate happening, (in 1874) having its inception at Aldrich, came very near to involving the first settlers in serious trouble with the Indians. A large band of 200 Pillager Indians were encamped near Aldrich. The station house at that time was run by a man named Costello who had, among other children, a boy 22 years old. A settler named Bowers had lost a sack of flour and located it in the tepee of two Indian boys. The Indians claimed Costello had sold them the flour and so demanded their money back. They were beaten instead. Going to their camp they returned to the section house with their older brother who demanded indemnity from Costello for injury to his younger brothers. The elder Costello ordered them off, but the oldest Indian stood his ground. He was put out by force. A few feet from the section house he turned and fired. The bullet took a finger from the hand of the elder Costello and passing into the house, struck Sarah Costello, a girl 13 years old, in the head, killing her instantly. Young Costello then fired at the Indian several times. The Indian was hit once, the fall breaking his collarbone and passing through his lungs. He escaped to the woods. The alarm was given in Wadena. Sheriff A.A. Wheeler took ten men, among them Joseph Swindlehurst, H.W. Fuller, L.A. Paddock and L.S. Pratt and visited the Indians tepee, but the wounded Indian had not come in yet. Sheriff Wheeler remained that night with the Indians, but the rest of the force returned to Wadena. That night the Indians held a council and decided not to give up the wounded Indian. Sheriff McKay of Brainerd, in the meantime had started across country with a posse, among them Slippery Bill, Marshall of Brainerd, and 32 men. The Wadena Posse again set out for the Indian camp and joined the Brainerd posse at the Red Eye. The Indians had taken up quarters in McDonald's deserted logging camp. The Whites reconnoitered the Indian camp all night. While the squaws ran bullets, Indian scouts were frequently seen through the night also. L.A. Paddock, whose sister, Mrs. McNanny, had previously been held a captive by Indians in southern Minnesota, and whose brother had been killed by

*Aldrich is located seven miles west of Staples on U.S. Hwy 10.

Indians on his way from Bismarck to the Black Hills, hated the Indians most cordially. He was an expert rifle shot and insisted on attacking. During the night the Indians allowed two whites to enter the camp and see the wounded Indian. He was lying on a blanket and two squaws were sucking his wounds with their mouths. When Slippery Bill tried to enter an Indian pushed him backward with an oath and at the point of a rifle held against his stomach. Slippery Bill was a noted character who had instigated, it is said, the lynching of an Indian in front of the Last Turn Saloon in Brainerd a little while earlier. The Indians despised him. Negotiations proceeded throughout the night between the sheriff and the chief, who talked through an interpreter, One Santerre, a Frenchman, who lived with the Indians and who stood high in the estimation of the chief. The Whites, being outnumbered two to one by the Indians, and not being so well armed decided to withdraw. The wounded Indian was never captured, largely because of the conduct of the Costellos, and because the Whites sympathized with the Indians, who had unquestionably been wronged. The wounded Indian recovered under the primitive treatment of the medicine man and the squaws, and 12 years later he was still alive at Leech lake. The name of the Pillager Chief was Miontomah; the name of the wounded Indian was Big Moose.

THE LAST OF THE INDIAN WARS*

If we were to ask someone from one of the eastern seaboard states where the last Indian uprising took place in our country – few would guess "Minnesota". But it is really not so surprising when we realize that northern Minnesota was about as underdeveloped in 1898 as any of the states of the West or Southwest.

The incident which brought troops to Leech Lake was in itself quite insignificant, and if a rifle had not fallen from its stacked position and accidentally discharged, there may have been no battle at all. However, the general discontent and restlessness of the Indians at that time made the incident possible. One might also speculate that the danger of a general Indian uprising across the lake region would have been much more likely except for the knowledge all Ojibways had of how the Sioux had been literally driven out of southern Minnesota fifteen years earlier following the massacres which had taken place in the New Ulm-Mankato area.

The center of the controversy was old Chief Pugona-geshig, called "Old Bug" by the whites. At the root of the problem was the illegal sale of liquor to the Indians. Government agents were seeking witnesses to convict "bootleggers" and "Old Bug" was being sought as such a witness

More recent action at Wounded Knee, South Dakota, and the Pioute uprisings in the 1920's could possibly be considered as serious as the Leech Lake affair.

Courtesy of the Cass County Historical Society

Old Chief Pugona-geshig (on the left), nicknamed "Old Bug" (The Ojibwe "P" is pronounced "B"). he was the focal point of the last Indian-White war in the United States. Although his name translates as "Hole-in-the-Day" in English, so far as we know he was not related to the Hole-in-the-Days of Central Minnesota, about whom this book is written.

The Steamer Flora pushes a barge filled with U.S. soldiers past the Lake View Hotel on Leech Lake toward the last battleground between American Indians and the U.S. Army.

for a trial which was to be held in Duluth. In his younger days, "Old Bug" had been taken to this same city for a similar purpose and was allegedly left to find his own way back to Leech Lake. As the story goes, he was twice thrown off trains. It was winter, and he endured many hardships, including freezing, before returning to his home on Leech. He vowed never again to be subjected to such treatment and this time he hid in the forest. Eventually he was forced to come out of hiding to report at the old agency in Trader Bay in order to collect his regular census payment. He simply could not forego what he thought was rightfully his. U.S. Marshals promptly arrested him; when he resisted, he was handcuffed. At first, other Indians were hesitant to interfere, but his cries for help and taunting words finally shamed some of the younger braves into attacking the marshals and roughing them up. "Old Bug" made for the woods but handicapped by his age and the shackles, he was caught again. This time a group of Indian women got into the act and "Old Bug" made good his escape. In the days that followed, a large number of Indians rallied to his support and the marshals, recognizing their own limitations and the gravity of the situation, requested military support.

Law and order had to be maintained and a contingent of soldiers was sent north under the leadership of General John Bacon and Major Melville C. Wilkinson. The author's father, Richard Lund, was living in Brainerd at the time; although only eight years old, he had vivid recollections of the troop trains as they pulled into that city on their way to Walker. Even though local citizens were apprehensive, they generally made light of the situation and cheered the soldiers on their way. He also recalled the somewhat relieved but very sober crowd that greeted a returning train with its dead and wounded.

The first troop train arrived in September, the second just after the first of October, and a third came later. On the morning of October 5, 1898, General Bacon, Major Wilkinson, and about two hundred soldiers set out from Walker on barges, headed for Sugar Point (now also called Battle Point) where the fugitive had his cabin home and a garden. The

Soldiers of the United States Army, freshly returned from battlefields of the Spanish-American War, report for duty at City Dock in Walker.

Courtesy of the Cass County Historical Society

soldiers spent the morning searching in vain; they encountered only a few women and children. At noon, a group of men were instructed to break for lunch in a clearing by the log cabin. As they stacked their rifles, one fell and accidentally discharged. Unknown to the soldiers, there were scores of Indians hiding in the woods around the clearing. One or more of the Indians apparently assumed they had been discovered and returned fire. The soldiers took refuge in the cabin and continued the battle. By the time the Indians retreated into the oblivion of the forest, six soldiers lay dead, including Major Wilkinson (for whom the tiny village near Leech Lake on Highway 371 is named), and ten were wounded. The Indians apparently suffered no casualties although it was rumored that one had been killed. It is to the credit of the military that vengeance was not taken. "Old Bug" was allowed to make good his escape to the cabin of his brother, Chief Red Blanket, on Boy River, and peace was restored. When the citizens of the tiny village of Walker heard the shots from Sugar Point and when no one returned from the fighting to report its outcome, they feared the worst and assumed that the Indians had wiped out the military expedition. They called the Mayor of Brainerd and asked that he organize what amounted to a citizen's militia to help them. Mayor Nevers responded and a special train left Brainerd for Walker. Dr. James Camp[1] was among those who volunteered.

Pauline Wold,[2] who worked for Dr. Camp, wrote the following account of Brainerd's reaction to the uprising:

> *Leech Lake was only sixty miles away, and Indians on the warpath might easily reach us! And with all our men and guns gone, we felt very much like "babes in the woods".*
>
> *Few people in Brainerd slept much that night. The next day we tried to get into communication with Walker, but the wires had evidently been cut, and no trains were running. The second day wild rumors were abroad that Indians on their ponies had rushed through town, but there was no news from Walker. On the morning of the third day Mrs. Nevers[3] called to find out if we had heard anything at the hospital, but we had not. Then said she had heard that there had been a battle and that several men from Brainerd had been injured or killed, among them, Dr. Camp. Not very good news for us! We were all feeling pretty "jittery." On the following morning a wire reached the hospital asking us to meet a train coming down that morning, and to bring soup, hot coffee, and surgical dressings. I must admit we were rather an excited crowd at the station. With sinking hearts we noticed as the train pulled in that there were several rough pine boxes in the baggage car. A shudder went through me when I thought that perhaps Dr. Camp was in one of them! Imagine our relief when the first to get off the train were Dr. Camp and Mayor Nevers. They told us at once that all the men from Brainerd were safe.*
>
> *Not so many questions were asked, as soon we were busy feeding and dressing wounded soldiers and trying to make them a little more comfortable for a trip down to Fort Snelling hospital. They told us that half a dozen soldiers had been killed, among them the beloved Major Melville C. Wilkinson, and that ten had been wounded. One of the boys had been shot through the thigh. They were indignant to think that some of them had gone through the Cuban campaign without a scratch, and here they were being killed by a handful of Indians.*

1. *Dr. Camp was a highly respected and well-liked pioneer physician in Brainerd. He also owned a cabin near the thoroughfare between the Upper and Lower Mission Lakes. A "pothole" between the lakes and the Mississippi River is named for him. The author's father recalled that the doctor's well-trained horse would allow Camp to shoot partridges and other game from the buggy and would patiently wait while he retrieved them or gave chase.*

2. *Wold, Pauline, Some recollections of the Leech Lake Uprising, Minnesota History, 1943.*

3. *The wife of the Mayor of Brainerd*

That evening we had a little party to welcome Dr. Camp. A few neighbors came in, and we then heard from him what had really happened. Upon reaching Walker, the Brainerd men found everything in great commotion and everyone scared to death. They heard that the soldiers, eighty of them under the command of General John M. Bacon and Major Wilkinson, had gone to Sugar Point near Bear Island in the morning, as news had reached them that 'Old Bug' had been seen there. At Walker a lot of shooting had been heard during the day, but no one had returned to tell what was happening. It was feared that the Indians were getting the best of it.

As Dr. Camp had spent a couple of years as the resident physician at Fort Totten, the men elected him their leader, thinking that perhaps he knew more about handling Indians than they did. So the first thing he did was to gather all the women and children into the Walker Hotel, the only brick building in town. Next, he placed guards on all the roads leading into town. 'I knew this was a very foolish precaution,' said Dr. Camp, 'for if the Indians wanted to come they would use their own trails that nobody else knew, and they would not use the beaten highways. But I did this to let people know that something was being done. I thought it might act as a nerve sedative-something they needed very badly just then.'

The Brainerd group talked things over during the night and decided to cross the lake as soon as daybreak came and find out what was happening. Early the next morning they got a large barge and also some cordwood, which they piled in the center as a barricade to hide behind in case of need.

At the 'Narrows' before entering the big lake, the party found a band of Indians, headed by Chief Flatmouth.* They called and asked, 'Where are you going?' The men answered, 'Over to Sugar Point to see what is happening over there,' and the Indians replied, 'We will be here when you come back.'

When the barge neared the point, the men went ahead very cautiously, not knowing what might be coming. Everything seemed very quiet, with only a few men running down to the beach. They seemed to be in soldiers' uniforms, but that could be a disguise and they might be Indians. The newcomers beached their boat very carefully and went behind the barricade in case they should be shot at. To their relief, however, they were greeted by soldiers and a couple of newspaper reporters who had gone along to write up the happenings at Leech Lake. A couple of more frightened men were never seen. They climbed aboard like two little monkeys and swiftly hid behind the barricade.'

*Chief Flatmouth the Second

Of course, by this time the action was over and the reporters had nothing to fear.

And so ended the last of the "Indian Wars!"

Even though the last White-Indian conflict in the United States took place in Minnesota and involved the Ojibwe, it is remarkable how little blood was shed between this tribe and the early Whites. The Ojibwe of Central Minnesota were proud to be called "Pillagers", but 99% of their militancy was directed against the Sioux tribes. During the lives and times of Chiefs Curly Head, Hole-in-the-Day the Elder and Hole-in-the-Day the Younger, only the peddler at Gull and Round lakes was killed by full-blooded Pillagers. Even among other Ojibwe in what is now Minnesota there is only the record of a trader being killed on Lake Pepin, another on Red Lake and three French traders who were killed by mistake on the Mississippi when they were thought to be Sioux. There was also the accidental death of the thirteen year old white girl at Aldrich. This is in stark contrast to Sioux-White relationships.

The two Hole-in-the-Days occasionally threatened to do violence to Whites, but they were only threats. On the other hand, there was a long history of friendship and mutual support between the Ojibwe of Minnesota's woods and lakes and the white traders, loggers, missionaries and early settlers.

APPENDIX

Treaty With The Chippewa 1837

Articles of a treaty made and concluded at St. Peters (the confluence of the St. Peters and Mississippi rivers) in the Territory of Wisconsin, between the United States of America, by their commissioner, Henry Dodge, Governor of said Territory, and the Chippewa nation of Indians, by their chiefs and headmen.

ARTICLE 1.

The said Chippewa nation cede to the United States all that tract of country included within the following boundaries:

Beginning at the junction of the Crow Wing and Mississippi rivers, between twenty and thirty miles above where the Mississippi is crossed by the forty-sixth parallel of north point of Lake St. Croix, one of the sources of the St. Croix river; thence to and along the dividing ridge between the waters of Lake Superior and those of the Mississippi, to the sources of the O-ha-sua-sepe a tributary of the Chippewa river; thence to a point of the Chippewa river, twenty miles below the outlet of Lake du Flambeau; thence to the junction of the Wisconsin and Pelican rivers thence on an east course twenty-five miles; thence southerly, on a course parallel with that of the Wisconsin river, to the line dividing the territories of the Chippewas and Menomonies; thence to the Plover Portage; thence along the southern boundary of the Chippewa country, to the commencement of the boundary line dividing it from that of the Sioux, half a days march below the falls on the Chippewa river; thence with said boundary lines to the mouth of Wah-tap river, at its junction with the Mississippi; and thence up the Mississippi to the place of beginning.

ARTICLE 2.

In consideration of the cession aforesaid, the United States agree to make to the Chippewa nation, annually, for the term of twenty years, from the date of the ratification of this treaty, the following payments.

1) Nine thousand five hundred dollars, to be paid in money.
2) Nineteen thousand dollars, to be delivered in goods.
3) Three thousand dollars for establishing three blacksmiths shops, supporting the blacksmiths, and furnishing them with iron and steel.

4) One thousand dollars for farmers, and for supplying them
   and the Indians, with implements of labor, with grain or
   seed; and whatever else may be necessary to enable them to
   carry on their agricultural pursuits.
5) Two thousand dollars in provisions.
6) Five hundred dollars in tobacco.

The provisions and tobacco to be delivered at the same time with the goods, and the money to be paid; which time or times, as well as the place or places where they are to be delivered, shall be fixed upon under the direction of the President of the United States.

The blacksmiths shops to be placed at such points in the Chippewa country as shall be designated by the Superintendent of Indian Affairs, or under his direction.

If at the expiration of one or more years the Indians should prefer to receive goods, instead of the nine thousand dollars agreed to be paid to them in money, they conclude to appropriate a portion of that annuity to the establishment and support of a school or schools among them, this shall be granted them.

ARTICLE 3.
The sum of one hundred thousand dollars shall be paid by the United States, to the half-breeds of the Chippewa nation, under the direction of the President. It is the wish of the Indians that their two sub-agents Daniel P. Bushnell, and Miles M. Vineyard, superintend the distribution of this money among their half-breed relations.

ARTICLE 4.
The sum of seventy thousand dollars shall be applied to the payment, by the United States, of certain claims against the Indians; of which amount twenty-eight thousand dollars shall, at their request, be paid to William A. Aitkin, twenty-five thousand to Lyman M. Warren;, and the balance applied to the liquidation of other just demands against them—which they acknowledge to be the case with regard to that presented by Hercules L. Dousman, for the sum of five thousand dollars; and they request that it be paid.

ARTICLE 5.
The privilege of hunting, fishing, and gathering the wild rice, upon the lands, the rivers and the lakes included in the territory ceded, is guaranteed to the Indians, during the pleasure of the President of the United States.

ARTICLE 6.
This treaty shall be obligatory from and after its ratification by the President and Senate of the United States.

Done at St. Peters in the Territory of Wisconsin the twenty-ninth day of July eighteen hundred and thirty-seven.

Henry Dodge, Commissioner.